ENVELOPED IN GLORY

TWELVE TALES OF MYSTIC EXPERIENCE

"And it shall come to past afterward, that I will pour out My spirit upon all flesh; and your sons and your daughters shall prophesy; your old men shall dream dreams; your young men shall see visions."
—Joel 2:28

John Curtis Gowan

1982

Published privately by
J. C. Gowan
1426 Southwind Cir.
Westlake Village, CA 91361

Typeset by Michelle's of Westlake Village, and printed by
North Hollywood Printing.

Privately printed. For sale by author at $5

This book is respectfully dedicated to two poets, Dickinson and Whitman, who wrote verse about mystical experience, to two psychologists, Bucke and Maslow, who were the first to examine it, and to two novelists, Herman Hesse and Patrick White, who won Nobel prizes writing about it.

The Presence of the Lord came unto me; My soul knew His touch and awakened. He made it bloom and blossom, and I was enveloped in glory.

ADVISORY NOTICE: This book is a work of fiction. The characters and events described herein are imaginary; any resemblance to any living person is purely coincidental.

987654321   ISBN   0-9606822-1-X

TABLE OF CONTENTS

PREFACE

When a writer who has spent his professional career producing non-fiction turns to short story writing, he certainly owes his audience an explanation. A number of reasons can be adduced. First, during his professional career, this writer felt that his energies, such as they were, should be devoted singlehandedly to professional concerns *pro bono publico;* to do less would have seemed to him a waste and prostitution of whatever talents might have been entrusted to his care. Now that he is fully retired and in a non-combatant status, so to speak, he has permitted himself, as a luxury, to try something in another mode.

The foregoing is, of course, a personal motivation, but the second is more altruistic. Since *Trance, Art & Creativity* and *Operations of Increasing Order* a number of well-meaning readers have complained that whatever message these works carry is often obscured by an erudite and prolix jargon, which makes demands too heavy for the average reader. They inevitably end up by hoping that a more popular book will next be forthcoming, which will make some of the most important points of the previous two but in a more palatable way. Since these earlier books were concerned with mystical experience, it seemed natural that the work of fiction should have that theme also, for while there have been many other works of fiction on violence, murder, sex, achievement and other human activities, there have been very few on this greatest of all human adventures. Since there are a number of different kinds of mystic experience, the format is a collection of short stories, rather than a single novel, — hence a book of short stories about ordinary people, each of whom has a dramatic and spectacular mystical experience.

For reasons of exigency, the writer concedes that these experiences are not fully representative of mystical incidents in general. Many such experiences are more interior and less dramatic, and hence make for much less interesting stories. In general, the lives of historical mystics seem to have less sexual activity in them than those we have recounted. It must be remembered, however, that most of the western mystics of history are Catholic, and that their biographers would have a natural bias for the removal of such material from their lives; what is rather remarkable is the amount of sexual material which still remains in such cases. Indeed, one of the sub-themes of this collection is the startling similarity between aspects of sexual and mystic love, in which the latter seems to be a transcendence of the former.

There are two other observations which need to be brought to the reader's attention. The first is the fact that most visions are intellectual (seen in the mind's eye) and not physical (appearing in physical space).

i

The second is the fact that a number of highly placed Christian saints and Hindu yogis feel that ecstasy and rapture are in themselves signs of theophanies which cannot, but should, be fully cognized, and hence must overflow into the affective area; in short, they are aspects of weakness instead of aspects of strength. A final consideration that should be made is that in Maslovian terms there are "peakers" and "non-peakers," and that here we are talking about "peakers" — those who easily have peak-experiences.

It has been the position of the Christian Church that mystic experiences can only occur to those far advanced in sainthood. Consequently, other types of allied events were generally condemmed, as it was believed they had a diabolical origin. The annals of biography, however, are replete with mystic incidents of poets, artists, philosophers and others. The first person to recognize that such experiences have a larger base than that of sectarian religion was apparently Maurice Bucke, who in 1901 brought out *Cosmic Consciousness,* a book which details 45 cases of "illumination" in both spiritual and secular subjects. Maslow in his various writings on "peak-experience" did much to bring to this area the analytic vision of a humanistic psychologist. A number of the rest of us since then have also labored in the same area. Indeed, recent surveys have found that a fair-sized proportion of the population can report one such event in their lives. Many of these are what are generally called "natural experiences" or "response experiences." They occur in response to some natural trigger, such as a mountain, lake, forest, stream, or other beautiful natural setting. Characteristic of these theophanies is that there is a vastly heightened feeling tone, though nothing preternatural is either seen or heard. Nature, however, is experienced directly as a part of self, and in a new light. Another example of mystic experience is sometimes felt as a result of accident, danger, or near death; these generally do not have as high a quality of emotion, since they are "forced" rather than "triggered." They may well involve telepathy, or out-of-body experieces. Perhaps the lowest form of such experience is seen in schizophrenia, particularly in the "shaman's sickness" (*dementia praecox*) described in story 10. Here the "placenta" shielding us all from ultimate reality prematurely breaks, and there ensues a period of "positive disintegration," a crisis, hopefully to be followed by the initiation into shamanship.

The manifestation of psychic powers requires the transformation of life energies. These energies are seen in their lowest outlet in sexual activity. Hence it is the theme of this work, and a common thread between the various stories that life energy, first seen in sexual activity and passion, must in some way be diverted or rechanneled so that it may outlet at a higher, psychic level. There is nothing wrong in sexual activity, except that for those who are called to escalate, continual arrest at this level wastes energy which can be used for a higher purpose. Upon analysis, it will be found that this theme in different shapes and forms recurs again and again in the narrative.

★ ★ ★

The writer is conscious that this explanation, like the preface itself, may be too long and scholarly for some, who, after all, may find it incongruous to have a preface before a book of short stories. But these tales are not merely meant to entertain; they have a higher purpose of popularizing an appreciation of modern mystic experience, by relating it to something everybody can understand, — heterosexual love. The accounts of such love in this book are not meant to titilate, but to reveal the power of passion therein, and thereby, by analogy, to indicate the similar power of passion which must exist before human love can be supplanted by the Divine. Whether the author has succeeded in this effort, only the reader can decide.

This theme that the "gods [of mystic rapture] come when the half-gods [of sexual ecstasy] go" is seen in story #2, (Paul), story #3, (Debby), story #4, (Alice, who has just lost her husband), story #6, (Marie), story #7, (Glen), and story #9, (Winston). Story #1, (Earl), is an out of body near-death experience, which often occurs in accidents. Story #5, (Anne), documents the fact that for a very few people, mystical vision is almost a common occurrence. Story #8, (Schroeder), and story #11, (Miss Tennoyer), involve very intellectual protagonists where the matter of the transmutation of sexual energy has apparently been handled as a part of developmental process in favor of the intellectual delight of discovery. Story #11, (Anthony), documents the place of the *dementia praecox* experience as a premature kind of theophany which, because it is out of sequence, has terrifying overtones. Story #12, (in concordance with the name of its protagonist, Egeria), is a "response experience" triggered by nature.

Mystics have recorded these incidents for centuries. In fact, the Bible is full of them, both in the Old and New Testaments. Moses, Enoch, Elijah, Isaiah, Ezekiel, Jesus, St. Paul and St. John all record them. But until our century, they have remained an anomaly and a mystery. It has taken modern humanistic psychology to put them into order and perspective.

Bucke (1901) was the first writer to give a semi-psychological explanation to the mind-expansion, which we call the psychedelic state, (Gowan 1974). His book *Cosmic Consciousness defines "illumination" as follows:*

a) The person without warning has a sense of being immersed in a flame or cloud;

b) He is bathed in an emotion of joy, assurance, triumph or salvation;

c) an intellectual illumination gives him a clear conception of the universe; he knows that the cosmos is a living presence.

d) a sense of immortality,

e) the vanishing of the fear of death,

f) and sin,

g) the whole experience is nearly instantaneous,

h) the previous character of the percipient is important,

i) so is the age at which the experience occurs (which is between 25 and 40),

j) there is added a charm of personality,

k) and in some case change in appearance such as might happen to one who experienced great joy.

Viewed psychologically the adventitious elevation of an individual into a higher state of consciousness, such as a nature mystic experience must be viewed with considerable interest. There has obviously been an excess of pranic energy, but why has it taken the outlet of bringing a higher state of experience into consciousness? One can only speculate that there must be some predisposing cause (high intelligence, poetic, artistic or high moral disposition, etc.), and an environmental "trigger" (nature, etc.) which produces a temporary escalation into a higher developpmental state, much as an encounter group may produce a peak experience in one ready for it.

The every day processes of living in the conscious mind usually succeed in the average individual in successfully compartmentalizing off the preconscious. But very occasionally, we find, for reasons that we are yet unaware, the upwelling of the preconscious area, like the eruption of molten magma from the mantle of the earth. This onset of active subliminal life may appear as the prepsychotic panic reaction of Boisen (1932) in those for whom its coming is premature. In artists and others, it may surface as the sudden shift in life style which overtook Gauguin and transformed him from a French bourgeois to a tropical castaway. Finally, in those already creative, it appears as a higher opening, poetical, musical, or even as a theophany or mystic ecstasy.

From our individual conscious view, a psychedelic experience is an episode when the doors of the preconscious swing open and the conscious mind finds itself master in a new and enlarged domain, with awe and exaltation resulting from new insights and expanded control. From the preconscious side, the phenomenon can be viewed as a final breaking through into consciousness of psychic tension which needed the fresh air of expression. It is at last full consciousness of the numinous, which is finally received at the cognitive level; it is finally *housed* in cognitive consciousness, which is its predestined domicile. The juncture involves both expansion of cognitive knowledge and emergent aspects of affective union, seen in the appropriate ecstasy. Blofeld (1970:23) says it thus:

> There are moments during life when a startling but marvelous experience leaps into mind as though coming from another world. The magic that calls it forth — as though someone had accidentally whispered 'open sesame' that rolls the stone back from the hidden treasure — is often so fleeting as to be forgotten in the joy of the experience . . . That the experience is not just a passing fancy but an intimation of something profoundly significant is recognized in a flash, but understanding of its significance does not always follow. A curtain hitherto unnoticed is suddenly twitched aside; and though other veils intervene, for a timeless moment there stands partly revealed a mystery. Then the curtain falls in place and at least a measure of oblivion descends.

But like the display of adventitious psychic powers, "natural" psychedelia is not valuable unless followed up by action and development; it represents potentiality, not accomplishment. Huxley (1945:68) is very clear on this point:

> Before going on to discuss the means whereby it is possible to come to the fullness as well as the height of spiritual knowledge, let us briefly consider the experience of those who have been privileged to "behold the One in all things," but have made no efforts to perceive it within themselves. A great deal of interesting material on this subject may be found in Bucke's *Cosmic Consciousness*. All that need be said here is that such "cosmic consciousness" may come unsought and is in the nature of what Catholic theologians call a "gratuitous grace." One may have a gratuitous grace (the power of healing, for example, or foreknowledge) while in a state of mortal sin, and the gift is neither necessary to, nor sufficient for, salvation. At the best such sudden accessions of "cosmic consciousness" as are described by Bucke are merely unusual invitations to further personal effort in the direction of the inner height as well as the external fullness of knowledge. In a great many cases the invitation is not accepted; the gift is prized for the ecstatic pleasure it brings; its coming is remembered nostalgically and, if the recipient happens to be a poet, written about with eloquence — as Byron, for example, wrote in a splendid

passage of *Childe Harold*, as Wordsworth wrote in *Tintern Abbey* and *The Prelude*.

★ ★ ★

Though the names and the plots of the stories are fictitious, some of the locales are actual. Story #6 is an exception to this rule since it is an account of an incident which happened to the author.

A unique problem occurred in the writing of this book, which, the author having solved to the best of his ability, needs to explain to the reader. In dealing with the extraordinary aspects of transcendental mysticism, it would certainly neither have been wise nor proper for the author (who has never had such experience) to rely on his own expertise. Instead, in order to give readability and credence to these theophanies, it was decided to depend upon personal report of those mystics, poets and artists who actually experienced them. Ordinary research usage would require quotation and source attribution, but this kind of procedure is clearly out of line in fiction. Furthermore, many of the sources needed to be modernized, translated, abridged, or otherwise modified to fit the needs of these stories. In an effort to avoid plagarism, and to give credit to proper sources, such material has been bracketed with footnotes at the front and end of each piece of material for which the author cannot claim responsibility. These footnote attributions are arranged in the "notes" section in the rear of the book in the order of the stories. If any others have been involuntarily missed, the author asks pardon, and suitable correction will be made in subsequent editions. The conscientious reader is reminded that many accounts of mystic experience bear remarkable resemblances one to another, which is not surprising, since they are all trying to describe one ineffable reality.

While not wishing to clutter up the stories with research information, the author is well aware that some minority of readers may be interested in further aspects of understanding some of the marvels herein described. For these scholarly souls, the section on "Notes" may be heuristic, and provide further corroboration for the fantastic in our midst.

One early reader has objected that "There is too much sex in a work purporting to be an account of mystical experience." The author, however, does not feel that he needs to apologize for detailing the experience of normal, heterosexual love, a common and basic one, and of all the emotions the one closest to, and the best preparation for, the mystic love of the soul for God.

There are in reality, only two love stories to be told. The first, which has been told over and over again is the ever-new, but always beautiful, love between man and woman. The other, even more glorious, but alas, much more rare, both in the happening and the retelling, is the impassioned love between the human soul and the Divine. These two are not, as is sometimes supposed, in antithesis to each other, but rather in some kind of developmental relationship and sequence. The establishment of this theme is the purpose of this book.

As for the definition of what a mystic experience is, we turn to a much higher authority, namely Evelyn Underhill, in her classic *Mysticism*, (1911:240-1):

There are three main types of experience which appear again and again in the history of mysticism; nearly always in connection with illumination, rather than any other phase of mystical development. I think that they may fairly be regarded as its main characteristics, though the discussion of them cannot cover all the ground. In few forms of spiritual life is the ever-deadly process of classification attended with so many risks.

These three characteristics are: —

1. A joyous apprehension of the Absolute: that which many ascetic writers call "the practice of the Presence of God." This, however, is not to be confused with that unique consciousness of union with the divine which is peculiar to a later stage of mystical development. The self, though purified, still realizes itself as a separate entity over against God. It is not immersed in its Origin, but contemplates it. This is the "bethrothal" rather than the "marriage" of the soul.

2. This clarity of vision may also be enjoyed in regard to the phenomenal world. The actual physical perceptions seem to be strangely heightened, so that the self perceives an added significance and reality in all natural things; is often convinced that it knows at last "the secret of the world." In Blake's words "the doors of perception are cleansed" so that everything appers to man as it *is*, infinite."

3. Along with this two-fold extension of consciousness, the energy of the intuitional or transcendental self may be enormously increased. The psychic upheavals of the Purgative Way have tended to make it central for life; to eliminate from the character all those elements which checked its activity. Now it seizes upon the ordinary channels of expression; and may show itself in such forms as (a) auditions, (b) dialogues between the surface consciousness and another intelligence which purports to be divine, (c) visions, and sometimes (d) in automatic writings. In many selves this automatic activity of those growing but still largely subconscious powers which constitute the "New Man," increases steadily during the whole of the mystic life.

Mystic experiences, such as those described in this book, are not the rare privilege of sainthood nor heralds of mental instability; they are out there waiting for us all to experience if only "we had eyes to see and ears to hear." When they happen to ordinary people like ourselves they are generally suppressed, because we do not want others to think we are queer. It is the hope of the author that this book may in part make them more understandable, hence, more expected, and therefore more often intelligently and usefully experienced.

ACKNOWLEDGEMENTS

The author gratefully wishes to acknowledge his debts to the courtesy of the following:

To F. C. Happold, whose classic, *Mysticism,* has been a principal anthological source. Also to Evelyn Underhill for the same reason. To M. Bucke for *Cosmic Consciousness,* the first psychological treatise on the subject, and still a germane source.

To Betty Hobbs for plot and editorial assistance and for the use of the poem "Metamorphosis" in story 9, (Winston).

To J. A. Gowan for the physics paper on gravitation in story 8, (Schroeder).

To Edith Garner for assistance on story 4, (Alice), especially the description of St. John's of Lattington, and to her friend, Dorothy Eden, for a description of Pepperidge Point.

To Jack Luckett for assistance with story 2, (Paul).

To the friendly people of New Zealand who did so much to make the writer's two academic visits there so pleasant (story 10).

To the memory of unnamed but beloved elder relatives, (story 7).

Last, but far from least, to my wife, Jane, without whose help, criticism, suggestions, forebearance, and love, this book would not have been written at all.

J.C.G.
Westlake Island
Nov. 1981

CHAPTER 1
Earl

It was a dark moonless night with heavy clouds when I went on watch as first officer on the bridge, and I steeled myself for a long tour of dull duty. Things were very quiet on the convoy and all lights were extinguished, so only the grey silhouettes of freighters could be made out indistinctly through the darkness. It was a time when one could think and reminisce. I gave myself over to it heartily as it was a good substitute for the war-time privations we were all enduring. I remembered my dead parents with fondness and the parental home in which I grew up.

I was brought up in a southern New England town in the days around World War I. My family were of moderate means, as my father was a traveling sales representative. With my brother and sister we shared a comfortable house on a tree-lined street in the upper middle class section.

Life was simple in country towns in those days. There were lots of open space for children to play, woods to roam in, vacant lots to play baseball or football on, and pastures to chase animals or better to look for blueberries or blackberries. There were Romeo and Charley Hill, the town coachmen, with their decrepit nags who used to fetch the occasional passenger to and from the depot. There were festivities at the various churches, but most of all there were the holiday celebrations.

One of these was Memorial day. Everyone looked forward to it, especially small boys, for cap pistols (sold early before the Fourth) were around, and their ammunition became more valuable than marbles and aggies. On the glorious day, a parade route was set through town, and nearly everybody participated, either as a marcher or a spectator. First came the police force (all five of them) on horseback with flags. Then came the High School Band, playing Sousa. Behind them came the three selectmen, in various stages of temperance, in the position of honor in a glistening Packard touring car. Behind them came the few Civil War veterans who could make it, all dressed in their uniforms, trying to look

1

fierce, but in the main merely managing to look old and feeble. Behind them came in marching rows the Spanish-American War veterans, then the National Guard, and so on down the ranks until the parade dwindled into a mere procession of private cars in general pandemonium assembled, but all with flags, decorations, and great good humor. The procession wound by, and stopped at several Civil War cemeteries, where dead soldier's graves were decorated, and then passed onward. Eventually even the small boys who ran alongside the band got tired, and only a few stragglers kept up to hear the Memorial Speech at the Civil War Monument. Then every one went home to baked chicken and ice cream.

My revery was interrupted by a rating who came up with a message. It was from the admiral: a submarine pack was suspected in the area and we were all urged to be extra vigilant.

Once again I lapsed into my revery. Memorial Day was grand but Fourth of July was something impossible for a small boy fully to describe in its glorious and smoky magnificence. For Fourth of July was not at all confined to the day itself. It began several weeks earlier with growing anticipation and hoarding of pennies, so that one could go, as a coveted boon if one had been very good, to one of the fireworks stands, set up in June about town and purchase (in niggardly payout, always measured in the pennies themselves) lady crackers, firecrackers, cherry bombs, torpedoes, caps, sparklers, Roman candles, and (if one's uncle slipped one a quarter) a real rocket. And of course, there was always punk, which a careful shopper could often get free with a large order of three dollars or so. Next would come the unbraiding of the firecrackers, which had to be done very carefully with a sharp knife or razor blade so as not to destroy the fuses which were so carefully interlocked and braided. No New England boy would ever think of the wasteful practice of setting off a whole string of crackers at once. It would make the Fourth go by too quickly. Then one would often seek out a friend and compare quality and quantity, making a few discrete trades to buy certain lethal items. One would also, as the great day approached, test-fire a few, (to the utter consternation of the dog), just to judge the effect. One also had to have an agenda for the Fourth of July to sandwich in one's private celebration among the parades, bonfires, pageants, tableaus, cannon-firing, speeches, and, of course, chicken dinner. It was generally calculated to put the whole neighborhood in a good mood for the rest of the day's excitements and exhaustions.

But the Fourth really started on the third. The night before the Fourth was the night for all adolescents to go to Nantasket or Revere Beaches and while the hours away dancing and carousing all night long. Others, like myself, younger and denied this ultimate freedom, amused themselves by an illegal, spurious and anticipatory celebration of the night before. Eventually, with few sleepers, the dawn arrived, and pandemonium broke out. The dogs were retired to the basements and everyone who had firecrackers was out firing them off. Girls, and others not so privileged by their parents, stood around in respectful admiration and just watched. Generally, after dreadful noise and smoke of several hours, plus burned fingers, the day-fireworks were exhausted, and the boys dragged in for breakfast.

At ten o'clock, the official public ceremonies began on a stage erected on the town common. All the dignitaries were there, flanked by military and naval men in uniform, a brave stand of flags and the veterans of the Civil War in full regalia. It was an impressive sight. After the flag was raised and the *Declaration of Independence* read to universal applause, there were speeches, prayers, hymns like *"Battle Hymn of the Republic,"* patriotic songs like *"Columbia the Gem of the Ocean,"* and a benediction. The parade formed up, this time with several bands, many more flags, and a much larger military presence than on Memorial day. It proceeded through town to the Civil War Monument where taps were played, and then all disbanded for dinner. In the afternoon there was a ball game, and fireworks in the evening. These were not widely attended, however, as nearly every family had its own fireworks display, and the whole neighborhood looked like it was under aerial attack. On one occasion before the ball game a man named Goddard, widely considered to be a crackpot, had arranged to send up from the common a large rocket, weighing nearly ten lbs. It proved to be quite a disappointment, however, as it quickly went out of sight without making much sound or fury, and Mr. Goddard was told not ever to bother the town fathers again. Such is the discourtesy generally accorded to peeks into the future.

Then there was the Fireman's Muster. It is almost impossible to explain to an outsider nowadays the full dimensions of a New England Fireman's Muster; indeed, even to explain why they had one at all is somewhat difficult. But have them they did, and there was a kind of pan-carnival spirit to the whole thing which may seem almost ludicrous to us now, but which was a very serious matter in those days. Civilizations have a tendency to make games out of those civic duties involving group activity, and one of these in early town life was protection against fire. In those days, pumps were operated by hand, and stout muscles were needed to force a stream of water into the air where it could work on an ignited roof. Gradually this difficult task of hand pumping on the part of eight, ten, or twelve men was converted into a contest to see which team could pump the stream the highest on their own equipment. Since most of these fire companies were not professionals but volunteers, and many of them were the solidest citizens who had the most to lose from a fire in their section, it may easily be grasped that contests between volunteer fire brigades, quickly became contests between the solid citizens of one precinct against those of another, and hence contests of high public interest, prejudice, passions and even a bet or two on the side. No self-respecting fire house could pass up this opportunity for glory, or a few free beers; consequently even in a muster confined to a single town, a number of fire houses in the different precincts were fully represented.

Fireman's Musters were held on the neutral ground of the town common in August or September, during a weekend (often Labor Day). This would ensure the maximum crowd and the presence of all the volunteer firemen. Needless to say, men who perspire at such work require food and drink, and the ladies aid and the various auxiliaries saw to it that a heavy table was laid under the elm trees at the edge of the common, though there was always trouble with the WCTU over whether beer should be served publicly. A way was always found, however, to get the beer to the men, and it was surprising how many men felt the need of it, though their exertions on behalf of the volunteers had been, to say the least, minimal.

Somehow, fireman's Musters attracted every kind and condition of medicine man, acrobat, carnival worker, charlatan, and other fast buck operator, including the candy man, the balloon man, the organ grinder and his monkey, the hot dog man, the salt water taffy man, and a host of others, who wandered through the crowd looking for their prey.

For some reason which I could never fathom, fireman's Musters always attracted Civil War veterans who usually came out in their uniforms and provided moral support. Whether it was the free beer or the fact that those who were ambulatory used to hang around the fire houses, they were always in evidence, surrounded by an admiring pack of small boys, of which I was one. They were not above playing to this adoring and non-judgmental gallery. I can well remember one of them, a small wizened man who used, in a high falsetto, to tell the following story on any suitable occasion, whenever asked about his limp and his taste for beer.

He had enlisted at fifteen as a drummer boy, and his mother had made him promise to stick close to the chaplain and stay out of trouble. He had always done so. One night on the picket line when he was with the chaplain, a Confederate cannon ball had come along and cut off a leg from each. They were rushed to the infirmary just around the corner, and their legs sewed back on; but in the excitement, his leg got sewed on the chaplain and the chaplain's leg on him. Ever after when he would go in for a beer, he would no sooner get to the bar than the chaplain's leg would

4

hitch him right out of the saloon. But one day, when the chaplain's leg had hitched him outside, he met his leg hitching the chaplain in!

The Muster itself was concluded in late morning; then would come the parade of the fire apparatus, and then lunch *al fresco* under the trees: free to contestants, 35 cents to others. After lunch there could be a baseball game. The carnival section would then open, and there would finally be fireworks at night. This was about as much excitement as a small boy could stand in one day.

Again my revery was interrupted by a rating with a message: One of the forward ships of the convoy had a submarine-like noise on sonar. Again we were admonished to be especially watchful. I put two more men on the bow, and then returned to my thoughts.

I did well at the local academy and matriculated at a famous Eastern college. Before I left that fall, my father called me aside for what was obviously to be a moment of truth.

"You are leaving home, probably for good," he intoned — it was obvious that the words did not come easily. "No doubt, you've had a lot of moralistic advice on how to behave; now let me give you the low-down facts, man to man. It's time you heard them. There are two worlds out there, — the floating world and the fixed world. The floating world consists of glamour and fun, and the fixed world of work and duty. And the difference between them finally comes down to one thing: —fucking. The floating world fucks for fun, and the fixed world fucks for family. We are all admitted to the floating world free, but the only way for man or woman to join the fixed world is to marry and beget and raise children. And now mark my words, Earl: the floating world can amuse you, but it can never bring you happiness; only the fixed world can do that. I'm sorry to have to say this so bluntly, but it's the truth, which I had to learn the hard way."

I sensed that this was a kind of summing up of the philosophy of a simple but honest man. He was trying to give me the benefit of his experience. I thanked him gravely, for I realized that the moment had importance. He put his hand on my shoulder, but turned his face away, as if he could not bring himself to speak further. And thus we parted, with much emotion unspoken.

At college I majored in mathematics and physics. Not surprisingly, I became interested in ROTC and joined the navy unit. Upon graduation I was commissioned an ensign; and since the depression had begun, I accepted the commission as the best job offer, and went to sea as a navigator where my mathematics helped out considerably. I did well, and when World War II broke out I was promoted to second lieutenant and assigned to a destroyer guarding the transport ships from New York to

Southampton.

Though I had never considered myself either fearful or religious, the long night watches on the bridge spent peering out into the dark immensity for maurading submarines were enough gradually to unnerve anyone. The trouble was there was nothing to do except watch and wait, — and think. The sea and sky melted into a black unity which compelled one to consider his mortality. They would still be there in all their unconcern and majesty if this ship and all about it should suddenly disappear under the waves forever. These distant stars had shone down upon planet earth long before the dinosaurs roamed it, and they were equally unmindful and uncaring should I or all mankind for that matter be wiped out like the great lizards. What was man's life or importance in the face of such verities as these? For the first time in my life I acknowledged a gnawing fear of the unknown, — of death and dissolution. I had no religious practice to sustain any belief or hope in the hereafter, no God to call on in the darkness. I was alone and mortal.

It was much better to think of my childhood and of other good times gone by, as I did, and to put such dark thoughts out of my mind, so far as possible. But somehow I knew the ordeal would come, and one night it did. Things had been unusually quiet in the convoy that night; there was no wind and little sea, when my reveries were interrupted by a rating who brought the information that our sonar gave indication of a submarine in the area. We got out our dark binoculars and watched the water especially for torpedo tracks. The last thing I remember was seeing a silvery streak in the water, headed directly for us. Before I could give the order to change course, there was a tremendous explosion, and I lost consciousness.

★   ★   ★

I became aware of a silver glow which shaped itself into a circle with a central focus brighter than the sun. The circle became a tunnel of light. Swiftly and smoothly I was borne through this whirling tunnel and as I went the light changed from silver to gold. There was an impression of drawing strength from a limitless sea of power and a sense of deepening peace. The light gradually grew brighter but not dazzling nor alarming.

I was moving swiftly toward a luminous barrier net, whose intersecting strands were vibrating with colors. As I approached the grid, the light increased, and my form was converted into formlessness. I was in a condition of being rather than in space and time. In fact I was no longer "I" but something more indestructable.

Beyond the grid was the almost ineffable encounter with the "Being of Light," whose effulgence grew as I went through the barrier until it was

6

unearthly and almost unbearable. I realized now that this radiance was the cause of all the luminosity I had seen but more dimly on the other side of the grid. But this light was personal, as if it was the manifested love of a Messiah which spread its benison to welcome the newly arrived traveler from earth. I could not look at this source of light directly for it hurt my eyes, but even at that I was somehow conscious that it was not a star like the sun but a living presence whose love for me shone splendidly.

Somehow I was warm and confortable again, though very tired. Family and older friends were comforting me. I became conscious of my mother talking to me in soothing tones, "You are going to be all right, Earl," she said, "but you must go back." My father was beside her; and other older family members and relatives, especially my Aunts, were in the misty background.

"Where am I?" I asked and then realized with a start that I must be dreaming, since my parents are dead.

"It's all right, but you must go back, Earl," my mother repeated; I saw her this time distinctly. She and my father were smiling at me as if they loved me and approved of all that was going on. "Go back," my father echoed.

It seemed as though I fell back into the whirling tunnel, dark and grey, spinning downward until I lost consciousness. But soon I emerged from darkness through the ceiling of a high hospital operating room, where there was an operation going on, with a supine and anesthesized patient and several doctors and nurses in attendance. I watched the operation which appeared to consist of the repairing of a head wound and other lacerations of the chest and legs. Still feeling that I was in a dream, I looked down at the patient's face. It was my own!

"Well, he's going to be OK," exclaimed the operating physician, then to the anesthetist, "How are his vital signs?"

"Just fine, here," replied the latter; "He'll come out of it in a few minutes."

"Someone upstairs must have been looking out for him," said a pretty nurse. And with that there was a "click" which was not so much heard as felt, and I again became unconscious.[1]

Sometime later I awoke in a hospital bed, feeling very weak and unsteady, and not willing nor able to move much. A doctor's kindly face was peering down at mine. "Well, young man," he said, "Heaven is saving you for something big. You're about the luckiest navy officer I have ever met."

They told me that the ship had been torpedoed with the loss of most of the personnel. I had been on duty on the bridge and had evidently been blown clear into the water by the explosion. I was very fortunate to have been picked out of the water, and they were amazed that I was still alive.

7

As the days went on, I was removed from intensive care and placed in the convalescent wing; here I had much time on my hands while still confined to bed. I was still weak and in a state of considerable shock. Nevertheless, I determinedly took some physical therapy to get life into my hands again; this took the form of knitting. I continued to strengthen my fingers in this manner and finally regained full manual dexterity by daily practice. Mentally, I also determined to find out more about the out-of-body experience I had had while on the operating table. Wanting to know if others had had similar experiences, I got books out of the library and read eagerly about the various kinds of OBE's. In a little while I grew stronger and became able to walk about.

After this extended convalescence in bed, I was furloughed on an R and R assignment to a famous ROTC academy in the midwest, situated on a beautiful lake in Northern Indiana. My duties as PMS & T were extremely light, and even though I was still somewhat incapacitated, I easily had time to accomplish them and have more for reflection and introspection. No one could have gone through the harrowing experience which had happened to me without some wonderment about the nature of life itself. I had indeed lost my fear of death for I had learned by personal experience in the out-of-body state that reunion and happiness lies beyond death's portals. But I was understandably curious about the mechanics of the OBE phenomenon and about further accounts and evidences of it.

I had always been interested in writing, especially creative writing. In the well-stocked academy library, I had picked up a book on automatic writing; and after becoming absorbed by it and its relation to the out-of-body consciousness, I decided to try my hand at it. I was surprised at how easy it was for me to put myself into a sub-conscious revery and how easily the writing came. I was disappointed, however, in the gibberish first produced. I decided to see if the quality could be improved by practice, and eventually I found that it could.

The Academy, an old, established and well-funded private institution, was situated on a bluff on the north end of a large lake in rolling midwest countryside, near the watershed dividing the Mississippi and St. Lawrence basins. For many years it had enjoyed an enviable reputation as a military school for upper middle class patronage; but, unlike other such schools, it had a strong academic tradition, with consequent entrance examinations, and delivery into prominent universities, as well as the service academies. Furthermore, during the war it had senior ROTC status, which meant that upon passing the requisite military and naval courses, cadets and midshipmen were commissioned lieutenants and ensigns directly. Naturally there was a considerable army and navy presence at the school, and every company had its own "tac" officer. There were extensive playing fields and a large golf course in conjunction with the 1600 acres of the academy grounds. In fact the school of some 1,000 students and officers, with supporting services, was a little city unto itself with independent lighting and heating and water services. The academic faculty lived in houses adjoining the campus on "Faculty Row." The superintendent (as was the case with many able-bodied school personnel) was on active duty in Europe; so during my stay there I was berthed in his house, which had been turned into a sort of USO downstairs and OQ upstairs. I used to spend my afternoons sitting on the belvedere porch, eating some of the delicious mess hall ice cream and looking out onto the bay where the white sails of the midshipmen's lightnings would race daily, with an occasional dunking for some unwary tyro navigator.

I well remember those bright autumn days, when the dry, crisped yellow leaves floated down from the large elms shading the many walks. Across the way beyond the morning sun and the flagpole, I could hear the muffled cadence of the drill squads, and later on the shouts from the football charge. One of the nicer aspects of the academy athletic program was that its emphasis was on the intramural not varsity sports, so that every cadet or midshipman was expected to engage in and be on his house team in some sport every season. As a result on Saturday morning there were often five football games going at once, with more participants than spectators at each. Of course varsity sports were not neglected, but a great deal of character building occurred in the intramural program.

I spent the fall in this peaceful and quiet realm, adjusting my life to the cadence of the Academy corps and enjoying the orderliness and structure of the military life without any of the brutalizing and de-humanizing aspects of war itself. The conflict actually seemed far away; my injuries were so serious that I could never be returned to active duty, and my surrogate function at the Academy was pleasant enough for my desires and important enough to ease any pangs of conscience, for I was taking the place of a military officer who could thus be freed for active duty.

As winter came on, I had discarded the automatic writing and looked for more conscious methods of inducing creativity. I eventually found, after some little inquiry that daily meditation followed by journal writing was an excellent method. Again it took time to produce more than trivia, but I persisted and was finally rewarded. My first efforts were some war vignettes, chiefly of the experiences I had had in the service or that had been related to me by others. In my regular visits to the library I had become conscious of the appealing quality of a young, dark-eyed brunette who was an assistant librarian. Her name was Ada, and she had been briefly married to an army officer at the Academy who had been killed early in the war; there were no children. My realization that Ada and I had some chemistry between us came one day when I asked for a book which was high up on some dusty library shelf, and she climbed up a rolling ladder to get it. As she descended, the ladder slipped and she fell into my arms. Her body was deliciously soft and yielding, and while I only held her for a brief moment, something electric passed between us. I decided to ask her to one of the Academy dance though I doubted if I had recovered enough to dance. I explained all this to her haltingly, but to my surprise she accepted with alacrity. We hit it off very well, and I began to take her to the Saturday night picture shows.

On the north side of the Academy, across the state road, there was a large wildlife preserve known locally as "the bird sanctuary." It was off-limit to cadets, but it was a beautiful, natural spot. I shall never forget one spring Saturday, when Ada suggested that she pack a picnic and we take lunch there. We wandered through springtime greenery, amid birdsong, for over a mile and eventually found a secluded grassy knoll which seemed predestined for a *fete champetre.* Ada had prepared a delicious lunch, and I had brought along a little wine in a flask. We ate our fill and stretched out lazily on the grass, staring up at the sky. She idly picked a flower and, one by one, stripped off its petals. "Look what it says," she whispered archly, giving me a roughish smile. "What does it say?" I asked, as stupid as any man can be. "Why it says somebody loves me," she replied, averting her eyes. I took her hand firmly; the realization had just come over me; "I am the man who loves you," I declared. She gave me a stricken look and lowered her face till she was looking down at mine. "And what are you going to do about it?" she asked, expectantly. For answer, I kissed her solidly. I thought she might object, but to my surprise she threw her arms about me and held me to her body in a tight embrace. And that was all the hint I required to make love to her right there on the grass. Somehow, our clothes came off, and we were kissing in each other's arms.

I kissed her breasts and let my hands stray downward over her body. She became even more excited and motioned to me that she wanted me on her. I placed some clothes under her buttocks and mounted her. She began to tremble as I did so and arched her back to accommodate me more deeply as I entered her. She breathed a great sigh of satisfaction as the union was joined, but the delicious trembling continued during the whole time until the last release.

We took our time together, for neither of us was in haste to end this delightful conjunction. My body was performing in the valley of a thousand delights, but my mind was lost in fantasy. First, I was riding a milk white mare through the sky that kept flouncing and rearing under my

10

spur in a cadence which overwhelmed me, for it was at once both spiritual and sensual. Then I was swimming naked through a milky-warm dark sea, whose essence rarer than water, seemed to enter my body and give it strength to thrust again and again into her soft, dark depths. Then I was flying in a balloon, riding upwards, and downwards between fleecy clouds in a sensuous rhythm which never seemed to cease. Then somehow all three fantasies came together at once, joining in a crashing crescendo of a staccato finale which roared onward to an inevitable grand conclusion, somehow obtaining instantaneous relief from the imperious enchantment which had overtaken us. Then little stars came out to twinkle as I lay gasping in her arms, while she sobbed and moaned in an ecstacy of relief. Then we tenderly comforted one another from the urgency of the ordeal through which we had just passed into some kind of purification, gently descending by stages from an exalted bliss. We needed time to return, to assure each other that all was well, and to reenter the real world.

Shortly after this we were engaged; and before the end of the semester, married. The Academy liked my efforts and I was rewarded with a permanent job combining the work of a military counselor with that of a half time teacher of mathematics. We settled down at the Academy, bought a house, and eventually raised a family. Later on I was to become a university professor, but this does not concern us here.

Needless to say, I have continued to write. After gaining an understanding of the connection between mystic experiences and creative production, and particularly their effect on writing, I began to formulate a theory about it and at the same time to search out ordinary people who have had such an experience. I have been especially interested in those who had been guided by such an experience to become distinctly more productive in their lives. Often, as was apparent in my case, this involved lessening of basic anxiety about death and a consequent freeing of latent creativity. (I must point out in all fairness that not all such experiences culminate in such benefits; for these events may contain dangers as well as be omens of progress.)

This book, therefore, is a compilation of some of the cases I uncovered in a diligent search, — cases in which the mystical experience was rewarding. I have purposely left out others in which the experience so frightened the person that he or she was unable to cope with its significance. I felt that the various histories pointed to some kind of basic mechanism at work.

Not only had my near-death experience after the accident removed my fear of death and the hereafter, but it also helped me to a dawning realization that especially with healing and creative writing one might be unknowingly assisted by friends and relatives who had gone beyond and whose loving thoughts sustained and even inspired one on occasion.

I began to sense there was some gradated connection between the light trance of automatic writing and the inspiration of creative prose. It seemed to be a matter of the degree to which the material passed through and was modified by the conscious mind of the amanuensis. Under these circumstances I began to develop some techniques about improving one's creative writing ability and to help others use them after I had found that they worked for me. Not only was I successful with several books, but I began to be in demand for speaking engagements and practicums on creative writing. But since that would take the story too far afield, I wish to end this history here for the time being, in favor of recounting some of the cases of psychic experience I turned up in my search.

One of the difficult preconceptions I had to get over was the prejudice that only saintly persons had mystic experiences. As a matter of fact, I soon found out that such experiences occur to a substantial number of ordinary persons, — folks like you and me, who live normal lives, are married, have families, and do not indulge in ascetic austerities.[2] Indeed, mystic experiences are far commoner than we imagine; one of the big reasons why we do not hear more about them is that those who experience them are afraid of ridicule or censure should they divulge them. So you will find in what follows naturalistic accounts of mystic experiences in all sorts of individuals, men and women, old and young, high and low, sexually active and not, indeed in all stations of life. We are all measured by our reach not our grasp; so it is not that these people lived ordinary lives with carnal impulses, but they sometimes, (unlike others), tried to surmount them. Let us keep this point in mind as we examine some of the interesting histories which my search turned up.

1 — EARL

[1]Further to the out of body experience, (OBE), see Gowan (1974:16-27).

[2]Further to this point, see the survey of mystic experience in the general public by Greely A.M. and McCready, W.C. *Sociology of Mystic Ecstasy* as quoted in Gowan (1975:391) which found that 39% had some type of experience.

CHAPTER 2
Debbie

My name is Deborah Lewin, 33, and unmarried, the daughter of a dentist father and a school teacher mother. The only child of a somewhat late marriage, I was probably overprotected and lived a quiet and uneventful life during childhood and adolescence. My parents saw to it that I had the best education, and I was duly graduated from Mills College with a summa in history. I wore glasses, studied hard, and was not popular as I was considered a grind. Then I went to Berkeley to work on a master's degree in archeology. I had become fascinated with the pre-Columbian civilization of the Maya in Yucatan, whose ruins I had first seen when taken there on a Christmas trip by my parents.

While I was there at grad school a very traumatic experience occurred which colored my outlook on men and marriage considerably. Having come from a sheltered home, I had had no real experience with boys or sex, outside of a little petting and a few well-chaperoned dates. At grad school I went in for recreational swimming, and since we girls did not have a separate pool, we swam after hours in the men's gym. One late afternoon, I was the last one in the pool when I realized that all the others had gone. I hastened to get out and dry myself when one of the male coaches approached me and asked if I would like to weigh in on the scales. For some stupid reason I agreed, and we entered a small office where there was a weighing scale. But no sooner had I removed my robe and got onto it, then the man grabbed me from behind and pushed me into an even smaller office. Locking the door, he informed me that he was going to rape me and that it would do no good to scream as we were the only two people left in the building.

Horrified and panic-stricken, I pleaded with him, telling him that I was a virgin; he only laughed and pulled off my suit as he pushed me down onto the training table. I tried to fight him off, but he was much too big and strong for me; and pushing my legs up over my head, he burried his face between them and began to kiss me. I was paralyzed with terror and moreover revolted to find that I was actually enjoying what he was doing, for it evoked a kind of pleasure I had never known before. I was only able to withstand a few minutes of such intense excitation; and all at once with a dreadful yell, I had a convulsive orgasm.

"Now it's my turn!" he exulted, and, grabbing my ankles with his hands, he thrust my legs over my head, and mounted me, forcing himself deep inside. I screamed with the hurt and penetration; but soon it felt better, and I found my body responding to each thrust. Deeper and deeper he went, until I could stand it no longer, and with a yell, I had another climax. But still he was not through with me.

Placing me on my knees and forcing my shoulders down on the table, he savagely thrust into me from behind, pulling my arms back and holding them for extra leverage. His thrusts achieved maximum penetration in this manner, and I thought he would reach clear up to my throat. I was in abject surrender, and completely in his power. Moaning and crying, I could not stand such intensity long, and began another spasm. Then I realized that he was having one too, and this somehow produced a final violent orgasm in me.

With a hurried admonition that I was never to tell anyone about this, he dressed and left me sobbing and undone, physically and mentally. After a while I slowly dressed and went back to my room where I fell asleep.

It would be difficult to sort out my subsequent emotions, so varied and so ambivalent. On the one hand I hated the man for what he had done to me. On the other hand, a strange part of me was almost grateful to him. I was curiously proud of my ability to act as a complete woman, but equally revolted by the crudity and power of emotions and reactions, which, until that time, I could never have owned as mine or felt could be aroused in me in such a base and dreadful manner. I became aware that I was a walking time-bomb of sexual passion and that I could never be satisfied with just any kind of sexual performance — I needed a real man — one not likely to be found again. Eventually, after the terror of pregnancy had passed with the onset of my next period, I realized that this whole area was far too dangerous for me to experiment with again.

The whole incident left me troubled and distressed. I thought of taking the man to court for rape, but even in that I was assailed by doubt. Had I invited his advances in any way? — Perhaps even unconsciously? And how about the most troubling aspect of the matter — my strong response to being so utterly ravished? Did my body know things my mind did not? Had it, in reality been ready for such an encounter? These cruel fantasies preyed on me so that I had trouble sleeping. One night I even had a dream in which I and not the man was the seducer. I determined to go for psychological counseling.

Dr. Mildred Thresher, my therapist, was very sympathetic, but realistic too. "I cannot advise you to go ahead with a prosecution for rape," she counseled. "There were no witnesses; no one heard your outcry. You did not report immediately to a doctor; there is no physical evidence; in the last analysis, it would be your word against his."

I told her honestly of my ambivalent feelings at the time. "You would be torn to pieces under cross-examination," she responded. A woman who finds any satisfaction in a rape is presumed by most male jurors to be asking for it."

"I realize that I have a weak case," I rejoined, "but this man should be brought to justice; isn't there something I should do?"

"We may be able to do something about him through private university channels," she replied. "But in your case, my advice is that you drop out of graduate school for a semester to get your life into perspective again. I'll recommend a medical withdrawal which will save your grade-point average; and you can start in again when you are more put together and can devote yourself fully to study."

By fortuitous circumstance, I learned in my archaeology department of an expedition imminently departing by ship for Guatamala to work on some newly discovered sites at Peten. It held promise for a release from the trauma of the past and seemed a wonderful way to acquire field experience which might prove invaluable. I signed up as an assistant and in a few weeks we were on our way to the site. I could not help remembering, however, a somewhat equivocal remark that Dr. Thresher made at the conclusion of the interview. "An experience of this kind leaves a trauma for some time; it will be some while before you can bring yourself to think about love with a man again. In some cases, it never comes, but the human mind has many ways of coping with stress and of transcending trauma."

In some strange way the sea was very comforting. I loved to stand for hours on the after deck and watch the waves and wake. Sometimes it was calm and limitless; sometimes it was fierce and tumultous; but always it was grand, all-encompassing, unifying and majestic, leading one to a therapeutic introspection, and a proper sense of proportion of the littleness of all things human. I found the sea is so immediate; it strips away all the ancilliary structures with which we fence ourselves in from reality; it has so much ground and so little figure. It inclined me to poetry. I could see Tennyson's "The wrinkled sea beneath him crawls" by merely looking downward. And Rimsky-Korsakov's themes from "The Sea and the Vessel of Sinbad" kept humming through my mind. The clean salt feeling, which somehow had a touch of mysticism in it overwhelmed me, purified my mind, and blotted dark previous thoughts from my attention. My dreams became less filled with terror, violence, and sex and once again were sweet and normal. I was cleansed and whole again. I began to enjoy my fellow colleagues and to make friends with men and women alike. But though some of my male companions became sexually interested in me, I begged off from any physical attachment or intimacy. Besides making friends, I contented myself with the inspection of the gear we were to use, and began to understand some of the intricacies of site work.

One night on the voyage I had a curious dream. It was totally unlike any other I had ever had, being so much more real and vivid. I could not get it out of my mind in the days following. I found myself somehow in the middle of a large enclosure filled with shortly-cropped grass, as if sheep had recently grazed there. The meadow was filled here and there with large upright stones, something like gravestones, only much larger, and not with that kind of cemetery feeling. It was solemn, something like an outdoor courtyard, with its leveled grassy expanse. On these stones were inscriptions I could not read, and some carried pictures of people I had never seen. I wandered through this magic realm like Alice in Wonderland; there was no fear in my mind, though I was all alone; it was as if a courtly entourage had just departed. I walked over to one side and there came upon a peculiarly shaped and angled ball court unlike anything I had ever seen. There were players there with plumes and feathers, but naked otherwise except for loin cloths. They were running to and fro with some kind of a ball. Then I woke up; but the strong, solemn but not unpleasant impression remained.

We landed in a small port on Guatamala's west coast and laboriously made our way on the Pan American highway to Guatamala City where we rested for a few days, before engaging trucks to carry the gear and baggage to Peten and getting the air tickets to fly there ourselves. We left on a rickety plane which had no seat belts and landed at our staging position near a large lake. There we stayed for a few days until the truck caravan caught up with us. Then we went on location at the digs.

Peten is a very large archeological area, evidently an important Mayan capital with many sites and buildings, a lot of which are still unexcavated. It is situated on a low, level plain often with stifling heat and humidity. But one would never realize the fact when first sighting the place, for it looks like a series of large earthen mounds, like drumlins left by the glacier. What is very difficult to envisage is that each of these mounds, underneath the dustfall, debris, and vegetation of centuries, is really a temple or other building in the form of a pyramid, which, during more than a millenium of neglect has become overrun by the jungle. Our party was assigned a comparatively limited space on the flat in front of such a mound. It had been found that the area on the front side of a temple frequently contained broken artifacts and other interesting debris which were worthy of rescue before the serious work of excavating the temple itself buried this section forever. Within this small area, each of us was assigned a couple of square yards, which literally had to be sifted over with a large spoon-like sieve. Naturally we made very slow progress, but even at that our endeavors were often rewarded with finds of beads, jewelry, amulets, broken pottery shards, and other evidences of a high culture.

On site I was harassed again by another male companion, — this time my straw boss, who did not see why I would not sleep with him. "One of the reasons for bringing along girls," he informed me, "Is to take care of the men, so we will not have to consort with the native women, most of whom are diseased." While he was not unattractive, I found this attitude revolting, and decided to talk to the expedition leader about it. Dr. Smythes, with his white beard and kindly face, was a real father figure to us all. He had once been a minister, before getting a degree in archaeology, and was a man we all loved and trusted. He listened gravely to my complaint.

"You must realize, my dear, that it is natural for young men to make passes at pretty women, particularly when they are cooped up here on site for some weeks."

"But, he said I was supposed to . . . " I responded. "Is that the real reason female members are recruited?"

"Of course not," he replied evenly, "But you must realize that some of that sort of thing always goes on at times like this; all this with the approval of both parties, you understand."

"Do I need to do that?" I asked.

"Of course not," he reassured me. "As a matter of fact the digs affect different people in different ways. For some it is an opportunity for sexual freedom. But for others, and I suspect you are one of them, as am I, there is some kind of a sacred aspect about these ancient temples, which makes this sort of behavior inappropriate at such a place. These monuments were their religious shrines, and we should no more violate such holy ground by that sort of behavior, then we would expect them to have sexual relations in one of our churches. Furthermore, I have always rather welcomed the enforced celibacy of an expedition to such a place, as it seems to call forth higher outlets of energy. I could tell you some strange stories about my experiences on sites. It is possible that if you remain chaste, this also may happen to you."

Only later at Copan, did I finally understand the full import of his wise words.

I had been for some months at the digs near Peten, assisting a large team with the identification of artifacts which were being recovered from a newly discovered side site. On an R & R furlough from my jungle duties,

I had come down to San Pedro de Sula for a few days rest.

One of my male companions had tried to inveigle me into shacking up with him at a Belize beach hideaway, but in line with my previous attitudes, I had refused, though I rather liked him.

San Pedro was a large commercial city with a bustling fruit trade, much of it for export. It is surrounded by banana plantations and serves as an entry port for the growers there. There was a beautiful old colonial cathedral, reminiscent of grander Spanish days. After one day's sightseeing and a visit to the banana plantation near the airport, there seemed little to do except to drink rum and coke and play cards, none of which appealed much to me. So when I heard that one of our party was to take a short trip up-country to Copan, almost on a whim I eagerly joined in.

The trip in a rickety plane (which also carried goats in the baggage section) was fortunately uneventful, though we landed in what looked like an upland cow-pasture. The pilots immediately hung hammocks and went to sleep under the wings. Then the soft-spoken guide took about a dozen of us for a tour to the nearby ruins.

The main court was a quarter-mile square, filled with short green grass, evidently cropped by sheep. The meadow was filled with large funary stelae, one of which represented a female ruler, another with oriental features, and another with a distinctly Nordic beard and Viking appearance. Around this enclosure at the South end were ruins of beautiful temples. Down below was the large ball-court, still in well preserved condition, rising above which was a long and magnificently carved staircase, covered with engraved bas-reliefs, which led up to a ruined library. The lovely meadow was shadowed by large spreading trees which gave welcome relief from the hot sun. Above the ball court on the other side were several long terraces, all ornamented in bas-relief, showing many nations of the Maya in convention assembled.

I cannot adequately explain what happened next, — the magical experience which came over me upon viewing this mystical and mysterious site, so much more beautiful than I had been given to imagine. A greenness which was something more than ordinary color overtook and overwhelmed me. It was like seeing Brigadoon come to life. There was a pristine order and connectedness to the place, connecting it not only to present time, but to the past, also.

It was not only the present Copan I saw, it was the once and future Copan as well. The grey stelae, each marked with great detail, with the erection dates, seemed as if raised only yesterday. The perfect ball court was waiting only the arrival of the ceremonial players. The beautifully ornate staircase mourned its Harvard-plundered capstones. The library, the temple on top — all seemed to speak to something inside me with compelling magnetism, touching me internally across the ages. I sat down under the shade of a large tree and lapsed into a spell. (I can call it nothing else for I was unconscious of time or ordinary reality). I saw unroll before my eyes, as if in some kind of slow motion photography, all the history of this sacred place, from the earliest days to its sudden abandonment in the Ninth Century. But it was more than mere history of which I was a disinterested observer. I was somehow connected to these people, to their emotions and desires. I was part of their culture, and I understood it as never before. I joined with them in this revery and became as one with them. I was transfixed by this vision, which showed the beautiful verdant landscape still yet moving. For something about distances became plastic; they were both longer and shorter than under ordinary circumstances.

How long I would have stayed there I have no idea, but I was suddenly brought to my senses by the guide, who, in a worried voice, was calling my name as he approached. He assured me that I had become lost or separated from the tour group and that they had been out looking for me. Apparently several hours had elapsed in that brief transcendental moment.

Needless to say, this experience made a great impression on me. I thought about it a good deal. It was so totally different from anything else I had ever imagined. I was not satisfied, however, merely to enjoy the unusual gift which had been granted me; I wanted to understand its dynamics, and I further felt that I could in some way be better for it, by putting it to some good use, a use which admittedly I did not understand.

So upon my return to California, I determined to find out if others had had similar experiences and, if so, what they had concluded. I was not too surprised to find that such worthies as Gibbon and Wordsworth had had "situs experiences,"[1] wherein they perceived the previous history of a special historical site, they were visiting.

It also occurred to me at about this time that such experiences, (if they could be made at will), would be very useful adjuncts to an archeologist attempting to decipher former cultures. I looked up "psychic archeology" under library descriptors and found that there was already considerable literature on such matters.[2] Most of the material had been given by automatic writing, although some of it came through mediums and other psychics. Deciding that automatic writing was an easier and certainly cheaper way of obtaining such information, I decided to try to see if I could induce automatic writing in myself. To do so I used autogenic training, a kind of self-hypnosis, prefaced by an urgent wish or prayer that some entity with knowledge of a particular site would use my hand to write. Naturally, before getting this far, I had made a fair study of automatic writing and its general relationship to creative writing. I concluded that automatic script is of numinous origin, and is generally non-materialistic and non-scientific, containing a preponderance of astrological and Theosophical data. It points to the survival of a type of entity which has learned material over several incarnations rather than to a quasi-Divine source which knows the information innately.

The first material I recovered from my automatic writing was little more than gibberish. I had expected this and was not disappointed. I kept on, always asking for a scribe who could give me specific information about Mayan sites. After many unsuccessful tries, one day I received the following message, embedded in a lot of gibberish:

"At the big lake, go away from Peten, and cross the river; into the country 2 hours, pyramids on a flat plain."

Many archeologists had suspected that there were Mayan sites on the opposite side of the river from Peten, but here were (if it could be believed) some directions possible for verification. To make a long story short, eventually I became part of an expedition assembled for this task, and we did discover monuments stelae, and temples in this area. (How evidential the message was I leave to the reader.)

I found that the information elicited in this manner was most useful when asked in a specific manner on site. For example one might profitably ask: "Should we excavate north or south from the pyramid?" or "Which is the pyramid front?" or "Are there artifacts or art objects buried here?" I had some dramatic successes in following up answers to questions like these and became in effect a psychic scout for my expedition.

I shall pass over other events of the same kind, but I would like to tell of an interesting extension of these powers, — that of finding missing persons. One day, three members of our party became lost; and since they had not told us where they were going, we were at a loss to know in which direction of the jungle to search for them. Again, I was asked to consult my guide, and again the automatic writing came back that we were to look in the NW quadrant, about five miles out. We did so and found them. Needless to say, by this time, the powers were well accepted.

There have been other instances when the power has been able to locate "lost" objects, such as a hammer and chisel left in a forgotten spot on site.

I am now on home-leave between expeditions. My next one is fascinating. I have been asked to join an underwater archeological expedition trying to locate what may prove to be Atlantis: Only a few fathoms down, off of the Bahamas, a stone causeway or foundation has been discovered. Naturally it would be very valuable to know what it was and which way one should explore to develop the site further. I am waiting for the final assembly, set to occur in a few weeks from Jacksonville. Already I am having dreams and images which so far seem unconnected; but I feel that when I get on site and can ask more specific questions, I will get more specific answers. It is truly a great adventure.

2 — DEBBY

For the mystic connections of automatic writing see Underhill (1911:293-7).
[1]See Gowan (1975:361ff).
[2]See "Psychic Search" by S.A. Schwartz in *Omni* p. 76ff (Apr. 1981).

CHAPTER 3
Alice

Alice DeWinter stood on the platform of the Locust Valley Station on the Long Island R. R. waiting for the 9:14 Local to New York. It was a warm spring morning in May, promising a fair day ahead. Leafy buds peeped out of the maple trees across the tracks around the lumber yard, and a robin was singing in the foliage. She glanced to her left at the grade crossing back to the neat row of little stores, at the rails themselves just beyond the crossing where the two tracks became one as the line dead-ended into Oyster Bay, and at her car parked in the enclosure on the other side. It was a good day; she decided she was glad to be alive. She did not miss Henry so much; or rather she seemed this morning to be more able to put up with his loss and the knowledge that from now on she would live as a single woman, bereft of her husband and left behind by her two children, now newly adult.

Henry and Alice had led a comfortable life at their nearby home, Pepperidge Point. Henry had been a New York broker; the house had been in his family for generations, and they had lived there all their married lives. Their two children had been born and raised there, but now the nest was empty and her husband dead. Clearly it was time for some change, but what?

The mournful whistle of the approaching engine roused Alice from her revery. She had better put her mind in order so as to talk with the estate attorney about the disposition of things, especially the large house. As she got on the train and settled herself for the bumpy ride to Penn Station, she kept musing about the old place and what was to become of it. She almost forgot that after the lawyer's appointment she had a luncheon engagement with a Metropolitian Museum docent about taking docent training. Being interested in art, she had felt that this service might supply replacement for the recent void in her life.

Pepperidge Point was an old estate on a tree-clad height overlooking Long Island Sound. In the early days it had once been the site of a sand pit, which had closed long since, the flooded pit now serving as a small pond for fishing and swimming. The estate included a nine-hole putting course, two tennis courts, bridle trails, and barns and tack rooms for horses. There were extensive lawns, and much shrubbery including exotic trees. The manor house itself had twelve rooms and required a staff of four, though Alice had dismissed all but her maid and a groundsman. It was built of stone and brick on two stories on the highest part of the ridge and showed a number of different styles, as if it has been altered and added to at different times in the family fortunes. From the entrance hall, one came into the large living room dominated by a central fireplace, with a picture of the ancestor who had accumulated the fortune over the mantel. There were two couches facing, assorted chairs and table, a grand piano, and oriental rugs on the hardwood floor. These were mostly Kirmanshahs, with wonderful pinks and blues which matched the draperies. The chairs were embroidered with pink and white French toile; the couches with silk, linen, and cotton chenille in beiges and whites.

The library was paneled in dark oak with bookshelves on either side of the fireplace and the opposite wall. The rug and the large couch and chair were in green, as were the drapes. The dining room, which seated twenty four had a cocoa-colored rug, draperies of English glazed chintz with an elaborate peach floral pattern on aqua background which matched the walls. A large Coromandel screen hid the doorway to the butler's pantry.

The more Alice thought about the old place, the more she realized that she loved it and hated to move out or see it sold to others. It was the last remnant of her marriage and family days; and with this sentimental value, it was very hard to get rid of. It not only had made a good home for Henry and the children, but it had been very pleasant to entertain the rounds of charity bridge, garden and other social clubs at the estate, and she felt somewhat diminished by the realization that she henceforth might be bereft both of the means to hold such parties and the place in which to have them.

She realized with a guilty start that such thoughts are unchristian, for we are after all only stewards of wealth; and she thereupon turned her mind to church work. Alice was a devout and faithful parishioner of St. John's of Lattington, the nearby parish church. She had always been pious, though in a somewhat superficial way. She especially enjoyed decorating the church with flowers and otherwise seeing that the transient amenities were kept up to the high standards of its lovely interior. Indeed, because of her large contributions, both in money and in time, she was chairperson of the decoration committee. She especially enjoyed flowers because their innocent beauty seemed so appropriate for Divine worship, and she loved to bring in white roses and mums from her gardens for the altar and aisle chapels.

St. John's of Lattington nestled into an irregular country corner, shaded by large graceful elm trees. The road at the left sloped upwards and the road at the right, downwards so that the two sides were at different levels with the main entrance at the front in between. It was high Episcopal, built in English country style by Morgan interests, which had imported craftsmen to finish the stone work and execute the beautiful wood carvings in the vestry. Stained glass windows portraying the saints interspersed the stone buttresses of the nave. There was a small transept with side altars with wood carvings. Oriental rugs covered the steps to the main altar, while behind it rose a large multi-colored stained glass window. Stone pillars and arches held up the vaulted ceiling with its carved rosettes. Wooden pews on a stone floor with their oval leather kneeling cushions had space for several hundred.

Although she had been dutiful about her religious duties during marriage, after bereavement Alice found her religion a source of even greater consolation than before. She prayed regularly for her husband's soul every night at her *priere-dieu* and read her offices of the day every morning before breakfast. These private orisons, in addition to the public ceremonies at the church, seemed to form a protective matrix or format for each day to fortify her in meeting her life with equanimity. But she found an increasing reliance on the mercy of the Saviour and an increasing tendency to think about His Passion and Grace. His presence seemed in some unexplained manner to fill, at least to some degree, the void of male figures in her life. She actually found she much preferred refuge in thoughts of Jesus to the somewhat snide insinuations of her women friends that she should kick over the traces and "take-up" with some of the perennial bachelors and widowers who, like wolves, prowled among the lonely females and widows in her set.

One night she had a dream which was very lovely. She, together with other women, was laying heaps of beautiful flowers around the tomb of, or perhaps a monument to, Jesus. Then His presence came to her, though she saw nothing; and she seemed to hear Him saying, "Feed my sheep." She awoke strangely exhilarated from the dream, yet ignorant of its meaning. She thought about it a lot and eventually decided that she should devote more time to her church work and perhaps work with the Sunday School.

One unforgettable Sunday in May, Alice rose early and, after gathering together a large collection of spring flowers, drove down to St. John's. She busied herself arranging the flowers in gorgeous bouquets. There were iris and snapdragons and forsythia in profusion. The vestry and nave were quiet and she was alone except for the sexton, who was making last minute preparations for the morning services. By prearrangement they did not speak a word to each other except for nodded good-mornings.

Having finished placing the flower arrangements on the altar, Alice retired to a rear pew and sat down to see how they looked. Heavy white brocade with blue and gold trimmings hung over the frontal. This nicely set off the four silver flower vases with maroon and golden chrysanthemums, specially grown by the local hothouse. The sanctuary had an air of costly and tasteful simplicity, which Alice much admired. She also approved of the soft, sandalwood odor, modest and not compelling, something like the gentle aroma of a rose-sachet in a well-appointed boudoir. The side door was open to admit the morning sun and there also drifted in the fragrant smell of the boxwoods which flourished just outside. It was very quiet and hushed, as it should be, though not at all cold. Alice thought how beautiful and appropriate for such order and tranquillity in God's house of worship.

Her mind turned to memories of her dead husband, and she instinctively knelt down and prayed for him. She then thought how selfish to pray only for those we love instead of praying for all mankind who are equally loved by God Himself. So she prayed awhile for all souls. She then opened her eyes and looked around with general satisfaction at the beautiful flowers and church arrangements. At such quiet times, when she was alone in the chapel, it seemed to her as if the church belonged to her and that she was the main beneficiary of it. This was particularly true when the pews were empty, and she had finished her decorating just before the arrival of the other worshippers. Great peace possessed her and she did not wish to move or speak.

[1]While thus absorbed in quiet reflection, she caught sight, at the side aisle of the nave, of a strange phenomenon. It resembled a thin bluish smoke issuing up lazily from the chinks of the stone floor as though from some fire smouldering beneath. Looking more intently Alice saw that it was not smoke at all, but something far finer and more tenuous, — a soft impalpable self-luminous haze of violet color, for which there was nothing to suggest the cause. Thinking she was experiencing a delusion, she turned her eyes farther down the aisle, but there too the same delicate haze was present. She observed the wonderful fact that it extended through the walls of the nave and the rafters of the building and was not confined within, for she could now see the landscape beyond. Yet for all this intensive power, there was no loss of touch with her physical surroundings, nor other suspension of her sensory faculties. Yet she felt happiness and peace beyond words.

Upon that instant the luminous haze engulfed her, and all around her became transformed into golden glory, into light untellable. The golden light of which the violet haze seemed now to have been the veil or outer fringe welled forth into a central globe or nimbus of intense brilliancy which cast everything else into darkness.[1] [2]Within this light there was a tabernacle full of splendor and above this tabernacle, seated in glory in His human form was the Savior, His holy wounds streaming forth rays that bathed the saints in glory.[2] [3]Above Him were the seraphim, each with six wings.[3] Above them was a rainbow of lucent colors and reflections. Then the Lord looked straight at Alice with a penetrating glance that went right to her heart, and she heard a small voice inside her that said: "Feed my sheep." Then the vision faded from the center outward, leaving the rainbow hues to the very last.

Alice could not at all explain the enormous impression the whole mystic experience made upon her. It was as if her very soul had been pierced with Divine knowledge, compassion, and love. [4]As she remembered, it occurred in three parts: first the theophany itself, which must have happened in the infinitesimal fraction of a second, though she was unconscious of time; then the illumination, a wordless stream of knowledge, love and complex feelings too sacred to describe; finally, enlightenment, the recollection of the whole complex, encased in thought forms and words.[4]

So affected was she that she lost her composure and, crying fell off the prayer stool overwhelmed with emotion and sobbing with ecstasy. The sexton came running and lifting her up, inquired anxiously, "Are you hurt? Why are you crying?" "I am crying," she replied, "With joy, peace, assurance, and the blessing of Jesus Himself Who has just appeared to me."

The sexton wanted to have Alice taken home; but being of strong character, she composed herself, and after a trip to the ladies' room, decided she was all right to stay for the service, though she was in an extraordinary state of joy and happiness. Nevertheless, later she could not recall anything of what transpired in the sermon, for she continued in a dreamy state of peace and tranquillity surpassing anything she had ever known before. After church, forgetting about a luncheon with several women friends, she drove a short distance to a lonely beach which opened on the sound and just sat in the car, watching the birds and communing with a restless blue-green sea. She then took hold of herself once more and went home, where she felt tired and fell asleep.

Being religious as she was, Alice found the impression produced by this unusual experience was a lasting one. It did not wear off as time went on. It not only fortified her allegiance to the church, which had already been solid, but it somehow seemed to reach into a part of her which had previously been impervious to intervention. She thought and rethought about the admonition personally delivered to her by Christ Himself: "Feed my sheep." She had obviously (so she reasoned) been singled out in a remarkable way to carry out some Divine plan, which suited her ability and station. She pondered a good deal on what this might be, and prayed earnestly for guidance. One morning, several months later, the idea came to her, clear as a bell upon waking, that she should devote her life and open her house to the subsidiary education of gifted children, especially in the arts, an area in which she was reasonably well educated herself. The more she thought about it, the more perfect the idea seemed; for it not only used her talents and strenghts, but also those of the mansion itself. The idea seemed like a Divine answer to her prayers and, like the person she was, she resolved at once to carry out the plan which had been given her.

Spurred on by the dynamics of the vision, Alice moved quickly and resolutely on several fronts. She called in carpenters for such suitable alterations to the mansion, as would equip it for classrooms. Several new toilets had to be installed to make room for both sexes, but fortunately the old rooms were large enough so that very little basic change was necessary. She wrote to the National Association for Gifted Children, and from them gained professional advice and names of local persons interested in the gifted. These together with some selected local teachers and counselors plus a couple of resident artists, she formed into a steering committee from which grew in due time a local autonomous association of parents. It was this organization with Alice's guidance and help which eventually organized the classes and provided the students. Alice also extended her efforts to raise money for the enterprise among her affluent friends. She led the way in contributions, but many others were glad to join it. In due time, her school, which operated mainly on weekends and for some late afternoon classes, became a model success. The number of children rose to nearly one hundred, and their ages ranged from seven to about sixteen. By inviting public school officials to see what was being planned and done, without any other pressure, Alice was gradually able to get them to cooperate also in modifying their existing programs for the gifted. She was always available as a speaker, though a modest one, and found to her surprise that she was becoming known all over the island as "the gifted child lady." Her efforts were noted first in local papers and then by a national organization, and all of a sudden she found herself in demand as a speaker in Albany and at national conventions for the gifted.

In connection with an application for a federal grant, Professor Hackman, familiar with curriculum in the area of giftedness and creativity was asked to make an on-site inspection of the school, and particularly to report on innovative curriculum to be found there, which might be worthy of outside support.

Professor Hackman found the school to be well staffed and run, with a good deal more informality and even outright happiness than one might expect. For one thing, there was a lot of singing and smiling. The former, particularly, was encouraged in class because it stimulated right hemisphere activity; children sang songs as they went between classes, and also in many of the classroom routines. There was also a great deal of art and poetry (almost all of it by the children) displayed on the hall and classroom walls. It was evident that creative expression was a significant part of daily study.

Concerning some of the more unusual aspects of the curriculum, Professor Hackman's formal report reads in part:

I. Genotypics and Biologetics[5]

A great deal of emphasis was devoted to an understanding of the development of the individual in all aspects — cognitive, affective, and phychomotor. The basis was the Paiget-Erikson developmental stage theory, with its five aspects of escalation: succession, discontinuity, emergence, differentiation, and integration. This was regarded as the carrying over of the quantum principles to behavioral science, and it was believed that students should study every aspect of their own development, including the physical. A great deal of attention was paid to physical and mental health, including endocrine intervention to make bodies more healthy and beautiful, and to maintenance group counseling to monitor mental health. A candid and explicit course in human sexuality and marriage was carried on in a very scientific manner, so that peope who all about themselves. But the thrust of these efforts was not toward sex or aggression, as with us, but more in the direction of the full flowering of the individual and his enhanced options and powers.

This impetus toward self-actualization was seen in several ways:

1. An emphasis upon a transition from formal operations (convergent thinking) to creativity (divergent production) in the secondary school years.
2. An emphasis on ego development and self-esteem in adolescents, but an equal emphasis on the fact that such personal development also involved ego-dispersal in the later stages, first in love of another, then in nurturance of children, finally in altruism to society.

Genotypics also included biographics, a selective study of the biographies of geniuses and creative persons, but with a different sort of emphasis than would be given today. Outstanding lives were analyzed in accordance with critical stages and the environmental. The analysis of the struggles of genius, especially in the early years, and particularly the obstacles placed by the status quo in the path of advanced thinkers helped the students to identify with these protagonists, and so with their problems, which were soon to become their own.

Shot through this entire study of individual development was the concept of consciousness, which was considered to be a major variable, though admittedly undefined. Nevertheless, it was in constant evidence, in discussion, in reference, and in thought, so that major or minor changes in consciousness and different states of consciousness were issues of the first importance. I detected three emphases here that were different from those I was familiar with. First, consciousness was spoken of as a singular which did not seem to have a plural; second, there was attention to and study of various altered states of consciousness; and third, the singularity of each stage of consciousness was seen as justified by the fact that there appeared to be a set of common percepts for each state which were dependent on that state, the percepts of the normal state being that of our ordinary physical universe.

II. Phenotypics and Ecologetics

As the first area, genotypics, referred to the development of the individual, phenotypics and ecologetics referred to the development of the species. As with the former area, the emphasis here was on flow and development rather than on a static view of mankind. Here, mankind was seen in the process of change, an existentialist view of being and becoming, if you will. Among minicourses, there were offerings in energetics (the use of life energies, including some we do not now understand), ecology (a better appreciation of Spaceship Earth and the conservation of its resources), utopias (from Plato to Huxley), futuristics (the study of and planning for the future), and species evolution (and the directions to which a few present geniuses pointed). There were also courses in social policy (especially a study of which subgroup each culture systematically persecuted and how this could be avoided), historics from a dynamic point of view (a la Toynbee and Spengler).

Another aspect of phenotypics was a thorough discussion of the creativogenic society — the society in which creativity maximally flourishes. There was complete knowledge about what kind of society and social institutions were maximally capable of producing each kind or category of creative talent. Particularly useful research was being done on the specific social sanctions which prevent or dull creativity in women. All this was presented and studied factually, so that adolescents might be forewarned. Peer group support through special seminars and extensive guidance, especially for gifted girls, helped to ameliorate the often severe social and group pressures against adolescent creativity or divergence.

III. Creativity

I was pleased to see that creativity at last had a solid part in the curriculum, being taught directly and not as an adjunct to another course. Among the familiar methods taught were those of Guilford, Parnes (the Creative Education Foundation) and Torrance, as were synectics and brainstorming. Further advances and applications by Williams and Meeker had been made, and autogenic training was offered, though this bridged into the right hemisphere area.

IV. Somatics

The area of somatics is perhaps nearest to physical education, though with a profound difference. Where ours is on group skills which often lead to aggression and team rivalries, theirs seemed to be on individual bodily exercises which reduced stress and contributed to health. While our physical education exalts youth, theirs was a preparation for lifelong body exercise which produced vigor in maturity and old age. The Hindo asanas, daily bodily exercises of hatha yoga, had been modified for Western adolescents and were much in evidence. Tai chi (rhythmic body movement which seems to promote meditation in movement) was also featured. But perhaps the most important innovation I saw was Reichian breathing and other unstressing devices, such as chanting, rolfing, and re-evaluation counseling, which were used for getting out anger and other negative emotions. These "hostillectomy" sessions were daily and even constant rituals for the purpose of immediately dissipating anger in the circumstance where it arose, for stress was not allowed to accumulate.

A kind of Orff *Schulewerk*, a chanting, stamping, noisy dance was also employed to reduce tension, exercise muscles, and establish learning through rhythms. Somatics of most kinds seemed to involve music. And I should add that there was much evidence of music and art in the schoolrooms, but I took this for granted in such a place.

V. Phenomena of the Normal State of Consciousness

The area of phenomena of the noraml state of consciousness included what we should call science and mathematics, but with the subtle difference that the name implies; namely, all physical phenomena were junior to the ordinary state of consciousness. There were minicourses in astrophysics, particle physics, and astronomy, so set up that they could be understood by nonscience majors. There seemed to be more emphasis on nuclear, subnuclear, and astronomical aspects of physics than we have in conventional schools. Mathematics consisted of more emphasis on exponential functions, binary notations and logs, statistics, group and set theory, and computer and artificial languages. Their interest in science seemed more open-ended, more willing to consider the observer as interacting with the experiment and more able to accept the nontangible nature of subparticle reality.

One new scientific study which impressed me was "synchrony," which, as near as I can explain, was a study of co-incidence in time, space, and magnitude. (I have used the hyphen to indicate that it was more than coincidence, although something like it.) It was also more than Jungian syncronicity, though, again, something like it. It has a lot to do with resonance on the same frequency, and the phenomena of sidebands and beats when the frequency or other magnitudes were almost but not quite equal.

In the area of scientific theory, I was especially interested in another shift in emphasis. Whereas I had been taught science as if the theory were true, these young people were exploring science to find out which of several alternate theories was most heuristic, that is, to see which theory gave them the most practical mileage in understanding and predicting the widest range of events. There appeared to be no thought or consideration given to the fact that one theory was "true" and the others "false," or that one theory was "truer" than another. This kind of freedom encouraged the development of independent hypotheses of which no one was ashamed if they didn't work very well. It also, encouraged mathematical but nonphysical models such as those of simple finite groups of three and four (which had much earlier been envisaged for quart models). There was also more emphasis on the probability function attached to the "truth" value of theories. This was apparently a newly invented statistic which enabled one to qualify a theory or hypothesis with the confidence level of credibility one should attach to it.

A final point that I keenly remember was that history had also been changed in emphasis from a history of politics, government, war, and battles to a history of science and art. It was evidently felt that the historical progression of ideas liberating man was more important than the historical progression of laws liberating mankind.

VI. Communication

Instead of language arts, there was something called communication. It started with communication theory, a completely different way of looking at the process in the manner of McLuhan or Chomsky. This was then divided into verbal and nonverbal methods. On the verbal side, it led to a study of phonetics, then comparative philology, including both foreign and artificial languages which some students tried their hand in constructing. Also stressed was the importance of meaning, the concept of a single semantic for each word, and the extensional and intensional use of words. The restricting aspect of language, as seen in tensed verbs which divide time into arbitrary parts, was discussed. On the nonverbal side, it led to a study of gesture, expression in the body, dancing, empathy, intuition, archetypes, images, dreams, ritual, and art

— all forms of interpersonal communication in the nonverbal mode.

A directive, intensive journal method of creative writing was universally employed, so that every student had a personal journal in which he wrote every day, often after a reverie or incubation period. The journal was divided into different parts (a la Progoff, 1975), namely daily log, stepping stones, twilight imagery, time-life dimension, dialog with persons, events, dream log, and inner wisdom dialog. Students became facile in self-examination and expression. Also, the journal served as an outlet and a confessional for those who need it. Its contents are private and need not be divulged, but they could be read to the teacher, counselor, or class if desired, and many fine pieces of poetry and other creative writing result.

The development of the ego and its dispersal in genotypics had a parallel in the categorization of meaning and then its extension to several meanings in a further study called "meta-symbolic calculus," in which symbols acquired several meanings and one constructed running prose, punning on the double or triple meanings. This is difficult to explain. It is a little like saying: "If you don't go to other people's funerals, they won't come to yours," which is ludicrous at one level but true at another.

The idea that a symbol can act not only as a constant but also as a variable, moving in meaning from one value of a parameter to another with change in development or social custom, is a powerful but necessary advantage of language. This enriched education took fuller advantage of this, thereby discovering generalizations such as "Bad exchanges drive out good exchanges," which is true whether the medium of exchange is currency, barter, or common courtesy. Such flexibility in thinking was developed by the "meta-symbolic calculus" that students were always able to see the forest rather than the trees and could deal with symbolic transformations with ease.

VII. Incubation and Imagery

Perhaps nowhere did the curriculum of this dream school depart more from familiar standards than in the emphasis on using incubation to develop imagery. The paradigm employed here is that when through various incubation techniques the dominance of the left cerebral hemisphere is broken, imagery occurs in the right hemisphere (similar to that on the TV screen), and such images can be transferred to verbal creative output by the left hemisphere, or directly to artistic output by the right hemisphere.

Incubation (as its discoverer, Wallas, 1926, noted) involves techniques of relaxation, so that the hold of the cognitive left hemisphere on consciousness can be allayed. Fantasy, reverie, and dreams are common names for the spontaneous appearance of this faculty, though these future oriented educators were not willing to wait for that to happen by itself but had developed methods for stimulating it in the classroom. As a matter of fact, I was told: "When the study of creativity was new, people tried to stimulate it through facilitating preparation, which is a necessary but not a sufficient condition for it. We, having done that, try also to stimulate it through incubation with phenomenal results — and this is the major advance."

Incubation started with laboratory work in guided imagery. In a quiet and shuttered classroom, musical records with various provocative sounds similar to those produced by Torrance and Khatena were played, and a few simple suggestions from the teacher sufficed to start creative imagination flowing. Some product, a drawing, a piece of writing, or a solution to a problem usually came out of these sessions.

Next came training in something called "withdrawal," although the nearest synonym we use for what was done would perhaps be ineditation. It was recognized that withdrawal from the tyranny of the percepts was the final step in the liberation of the consciousness begun by Piagetian "decentering" and by the freeing which subjunctive contingency gives to the formal operations stage over the tyranny of the present indicative in the concrete operations stage. Objectivity, according to their view, could only be found by total disengagement from the object, at least for a time. It was realized that different temperaments needed different methods so a number were taught, including Eastern and Western meditation, psychosynthesis, autogenic training, something called BEST, Nichirin Shosho chanting, and several others. Students were encouraged in the private, daily use of whichever one they liked the best.

Although I was much interested in this spectacular method of enhancement of intelligence I was not given much further information about it; it was probable that even they did not fully understand it. When I asked about this, they replied with a question, "does the fact that you don't understand what electricity is, keep you from using it?" I was told, however, that in a few precocious individuals such powers could be extended into telepathy and precognition, although psychologists were concerned about possible harmful effects of developmental forcing in this sensitive area.

VIII. Philosophics and Theoretics

The experiences involved in philosophics and theoretics were a sort of capstone, combining many other aspects under a common head. Again it is necessary to explain that students "played" with theory rather than espousing belief. Consequently there was not the personal investment in letting go an old concept and trying out a new one.

First there was a review of communications theory and of major world religions, but again in a very detached way, from the point of view of developing a repertoire of theories rather than as articles of belief. Then there was a study of general systems which saw all thought as unified in process under a diversity of forms and applications. Each science and discipline was isomorphic to every other science, except that it had special variables and constants. In this logic and mathematics played a leading part.

General systems were followed by a study of major paradigms and homologues which synthesized and summarized earlier isomorphic relationships in the creativity studies. Among those which were familiar to me were the complementarity principle in physics, the quantum theory of discontinuity, the Pribram hologram model, the right hemisphere analogue to a radio receiver, and several others. Finally, there was an introductory study of noetics, the analysis of mind and consciousness in which some equivalence seemed to be made between the inner world of the mind and the outer world of events and things, as if each were the inverse of the other.[5]

★ ★ ★

This abstract from the report gives the major curriculum innovations which were found in the DeWinter special school. It concluded with the professor's admiration for the excellent and demanding curriculum in place for educating the ablest of the next generation.

I learned about this school only because Professor Hackman happened to be a personal friend and related to me the strange story which Alice told him. His curiosity had been aroused by the many excellent innovations in the school curriculum and he was eager to find out from Alice where she got the ideas for this unique school.

She confessed to him that along with the original idea, which came to her in the vision heretofore described, they were given to her in several dreams complete with guidelines for curriculum design, content of study areas and a technique for implementing learning activities. She pointed out that she had read and talked with educators during this time, and felt that this cognitive input had some parts in forming the dream content. While somewhat skeptical about some parts of her story, he was forced to admit that there were uniquely valuable curriculum modifications to be found in the school. He found it to be one of the most remarkable stories of the blending of conscious and unconscious expertise that he had ever experienced, and while he was somewhat astounded by some of the more spectacular details, he had to admit that the results had been excellent and far reaching in their significance. He left the school with a profound admiration for a woman who had had the courage and commitment to follow up the lead of her dreams and visions.

Sensing that inclusion of any of the transpersonal material would seriously prejudice the application for funding, he had confided in me to see if I could agree with his decision to excise it from his formal report. I was glad to relieve his conscience by agreeing with him.

★   ★   ★

This enlarged activity in service of society did not in any way diminish Alice's religious piety, but it seemed somehow to be an application of it. Each seemed to feed the other with energy, so that Alice found that she was able to accomplish both with zest and vigor. But the effect of the vision was in some strange way able to project her practice of religion outward among her fellow creatures, instead of leaving it where it had been as an interior and personal matter. She saw each of the children as a prayer, each of their accomplishments as a prayer answered. Her faith was less concerned with her self and her salvation and more concerned with others and theirs. Through love, crisis and transcendence, it had passed from an examination of self to help and nurturance of others.

3 — ALICE

The locale of this story is real and so is St. John's Lattington in Locust Valley, L.I.

[1]This vision is that narrated by W.L. Wilmhurst in *Contemplations* (J.M. Watkins: London), as quoted by Happold (1963:p 137-8).

[2]St. Francis of Rome as quoted by Reinhold, H.A. *The Soul A fire*, New York: Doubleday, 1973:228 as quoted by Gowan (1975:366).

[3]Isaiah Ch. 6.

[4]From Allen, E.W. *The Timeless Moment*, London: 1966:30-1 as quoted by Gowan (1975:366).

[5]This academic report is from the writer's "The Education of the Gifted in Utopia" (pages 149-163) in Gowan, J.C.; Khatena, J. and Torrance, E.P. (Eds.) *Educating the Ablest* (2nd Ed.) Itasca, Ill: F.E. Peacock & Co., 1979.

CHAPTER 4
Paul

When I first met Paul Planett he was the very type and model of a successful young lawyer on his way to fame and fortune. His slim figure, long patrician face, curly brown hair, hazel eyes and prominent, handsome nose were enough to compel admiring responses from women; in addition, he had a commanding air, and a certain candid quality which made him a trustworthy source of authority in men's eyes as well. There was something equally hypnotic and straightforward about the eyes which bespoke both the power of decision and concern for others. Altogether, he was a prepossessing person.

Women, especially, were enamoured of Paul. He was so totally different, — handsome, graceful with a certain soigne elegance, — a touch of class which made him look as though he had just come from Brooks Brothers or J. Press. As much as women admired his ability to take command of the situation, they also liked his capacity to deal with people, his irreverence on occasion, his innate sense of humor and his boyish vulnerability. There was a certain dash reminiscent of JFK about him — the hero, as himself a hero worshipper — a compassionate as well as dispassionate view above the heat of battle, worthy of an Arjuna in the *Rig Veda*. Perhaps it was that they sensed the poet in him.

Despite his Ivy League air, Paul had come up the hard way, nurtured by talent alone. He had been brought up in a broken home by an Aunty Mame type of mother whose optimism about the lasting qualities of the next man never seemed to diminish through experience. They moved often, frequently living in hotels and Paul never did settle down to a normal bringing-up, eventually leaving high school for Vietnam service with the Marines. He was sent back for Officer's Training School, and eked out his GED and eventually college credits while in the service, ending up with a law degree and a Lt. Colonelcy in the Marines. In both war and peace he was like a Renaissance man, activated to do well in whatever he turned his hand to. By this time he had married and was the father of several children.

We shall pass over the intervening years since they do not concern the focus of our story. Paul became very successful as a lawyer, but his concern for human rights kept him from prosecution and seemed to predestine him for politics. He entered some local races and won, becoming first a school board member, then city councilman, and finally was rewarded by a seat in the legislature, where he was again a popular and influential member. This new job kept him away from home a lot at the state capitol, and the enforced separation wore hard on his marriage. Eventually there was a divorce, which came, as luck would have it, right during the political campaign. Paul was defeated. He had lost his law practice, his wife and family, and now his assembly seat. True to his character he accepted these reverses with his usual philosophic humor. But he was undoubtedly at loose ends and in the midst of a life change.

A friend suggested that he spend some time at a famous California retreat in the mountains of Big Sur. For lack of anything else to do Paul attended; he was surprised to find the message of peace, self-understanding, individual development, and freedom there promulgated. Many of these new ideas he had never considered before, and he began serious study of books by Perls, Capra, Murphy, Krippner, Menninger, the Greens, and many others teaching or advocating a humanistic and transpersonal psychology. These matters intrigued his mind with the promise of a new turn of his own development, though he was very unclear what concrete steps this might take.

Besides the ideas it stood for and the famous authors who came there to teach, the center was also famous (or perhaps notorious) for another feature. It was situated on a fault which produced natural hot springs, and it was the custom to go nude bathing for relaxation after hours in one of the many thermal pools. Needless to say these activities were great ice-breakers, and Paul soon was on first name terms with the remainder of the staff and clients. Among these was a slender, pretty assistant named Eugenia, — Jean for short. She had been in the mental health movement for some time and knew a good deal more about it than Paul did, as she had taught classes in body fitness and Reichian breathing. Paul found she was even prettier in the pool than with her clothes on. Furthermore, like many such women, she was thoroughly liberated and allowed him to touch and fondle her in the warm water. He had known other women, but touching her excited him tremendously. He wanted to be near her, and they began to have meals together.

One night after a long session, he asked Jean if she would like to go down to one of the more isolated pools with him. To his surprise she readily agreed. They walked down, arm in arm; she let him kiss her; and shedding their clothes, they entered the dark warm pool together. She came to him, and they played awhile nuzzling each other softly and gently. She would let him stroke her breasts, then playfully evade him. Soon, however, she came up to him to be soundly kissed with her mouth open, and wrapping her legs around him, she leaned back so that he could more easily kiss and massage her breasts. Suddenly his excitement came; and seizing her in his arms, he threw her knees over his shoulders and grabbing her by her upper arms threw her head back nearly into the water. She knew instinctively how he wanted her and arched her back so that her torso was open to him. In this position, he was able to enter deeply into her, and with each thrust to feel the thrill of her passion which this complete conjunction produced. Her ardor impassioned him; and quicker and quicker came his thrusts, and wilder and wilder her convulsive motions, until she could stand it no longer, and with a cry which was both triumph and submission, lay limp and contented in his arms. He tenderly cradled her during the magical moments of afterglow until she was somewhat recovered. She finished with a gentle crying; then she turned to him and covered his wet face with kisses. They remained in this blissful state for a longish time, with the rest of the world shut out, needing nothing else to complete their joy. Then suddenly the water seemed cold, and they parted, got out and dried themselves, gradually returning to the world they had left behind.

Paul immediately went to bed and fell into deep and blissful sleep. But toward morning he had a strange dream. He was making love to a beautiful female figure in an idealized sort of way, in that he was conscious of love but not passion. Their tryst finished she presented him with something. It seemed the fruit of their union, but it was not a baby; instead it was some power she bestowed upon him; it gradually became clear to him that it was the power to heal. Things seemed mixed up in the dream, and he was very confused afterwards about it, though it left him with a pleasant and warm after-emotion.

He was not, however, in the least confused about what had happened the previous evening with Jean nor of how he felt about her.

The next day, when Paul could get Jean alone, they went out on the grass to talk and Paul asked her to marry him. She said nothing for a long while, but took his left palm and gazed at it intently. Finally, she broke silence.

"Paul, I love you as much as you love me," she said slowly. "And if I were to be selfish, I would accept you immediately. But you are a rare person, and you are going through a great change in your life. Change-points are very poor times to make lasting decisions. You have a great deal of potential in the spiritual realm as well as in the material. I can see it in your hand. There is a possibility that enormous change and advancement will take place in your life over the next few years; you may become very different than you are now. You are ready for a genuine spiritual experience which could be earth-shaking for you. It would be unfair of me to bind you now to something you might all too soon outgrow. Let us instead continue to love each other but put the decision about marriage on hold for a year, until you can see more clearly where you are going, and what you really need. Right now you need to go out from this place and seek the Holy Grail; how it will appear to you I do not know, but until you have satisfied this thirst in you for the Quest, you are not for me or any woman, whether you realize that or not. Now give me a kiss, and let us part. I will always be here if you need me, after your Quest is over."

Something inside Paul made him realize that Jean spoke the truth. Without protest or further argument he kissed her briefly, went to his room, packed his bags, and took off from the center to spend some time visiting with married friends in the Sierras. Early one morning about two weeks later, Paul decided to take the car out for a spin. He drove through a rural area, dotted with flowering almond trees. A country road ran up a lovely valley, which was parallel to a meandering stream. There was a large meadow full of spring flowers between the road and the water. Beyond the far bank the sun had risen over distant blue mountains on what was obviously a perfect spring day. Somehow all the stress of the past seemed to leave Paul; he was calm and at peace at last. The scene was so beautiful that he stopped the car and sat down on a stone at the edge of the meadow to contemplate it.

The light had a pristine quality and he was reminded of Thoreau's statement that all the intelligences are alive in the morning. He continued to gaze as if hypnotized by the simple pastoral beauty of the landscape before him. There was absolute quiet; not another soul was in sight. As he sat there in the stillness suddenly and subtly the tableau shifted, — he could never recollect how afterwards, — and 'he saw in the light the river blazing with radiance. Out of that effulgence there seemed to rise a spring of water or something rarer, streaming upward in an etheric arc and then downward onto the flowers, issuing sparklets of glory that settled on each blossom and bud, like rubies set in gold. Then, as it were, inspired and inebriated by the floral perfume, these radiant streamers plunged again into this wondrous flood of light, losing themselves in its lambent brilliance, one entering as another issued forth in a continual streaming of light and energy.

With the onset of all this magic activity, the flowers became as if alive. They were vibrating in harmony, communicating their joy to each other and to the light itself, issuing sparks of some unknown rare and etheral susbtance. It seemed as if from each came gossamer jewels materializing from some enchanted and invisible realm. Suddenly Paul realized with a

40

start that the flowers were alive; they were praising God for His magnificent benison in sacred ceremony; and that he had somehow become privy to this celebration of innermost joy and exaltation. The words of Thomas Traherne came to his mind:

> [2]You will never enjoy the world aright till you see the wisdom and power of God in a grain of sand. Your enjoyment of the world is never right till every morning you wake up in heaven; see yourself in your Father's palace, and look upon the skies and earth and seas as celestial joys, having such reverend esteem for all as if you were among the angels . . . [2]

He realized then, more fully than ever he had before that nature is one with God and mirrors, though imperfectly, His perfection. And still the flowing, living light spoke to his heart saying: "The river, the carnelians and topazes, — all the scented jewels that issue forth, — the smiling flowers which give back the splendor, are but shadowly foretastes of My Glory, for of all objects in this transient world of continual change and perishing, these and these alone give us visible images of the beauties and harmonies of true perfection."[1]

Soon after this monumental experience, Paul began to realize that a life of dedication to God evoked a triple vow from him:
1. poverty (non-attachment to material things)
2. chastity (non-attachment to the glamour of sex)
3. obedience (not to a director but to an inner source).

Paul took these traditional monastic vows with modern moderation, not ecclesiastical rigidity; it was not the act of having things or having sex, or having a mind of one's own that was the focus of the vow; it was the craving, attachment, or lusting for such objects. The first was the most difficult since it meant giving up a home and most material possessions (except some books, a car and a few clothes) and living the life of a wanderer. It took a great deal of will power and courage to make this divestiture, but eventually he succeeded. Paul gave up his law practice, and wandered about in a car, staying with friends, or house sitting, and continually searching for Divinity in fellow humans. The sexual transcendence was not so difficult, once Paul realized that it did not preclude embracing, hugging, and physical closeness. But for the healing power to arise, the seminal fluid must be conserved from the ejaculation of intercourse to be absorbed by the internal ascent of the kundalini power up the spine. As in the case of poverty, then, chastity was less an absolute than an ideal, rather to be emphasized than to be observed with extreme rigor. Obedience, the constant listening to the inner voice was the easiest of all.

41

As Paul completed divesting himself of his possessions, perhaps the greatest change in him was the gradual loosening of the bonds of attachment. He learned that non-attachment meant the removal of any single object from one's aspirations, fantasies, longngs, concerns or desires. One must neither be attached to, nor desire to have or enjoy, money, material possessions, gambling, drink or tobacco. All these were comparatively easy, but greater challenges were to follow. Non-attachment also meant that one did not desire nor think about the beautiful bodies of women, — of their graceful slender backs, their full round breasts, their dimpled buttocks, their voluptuous bellies, nor their fur-lined secret treasures. But in renouncing attachment to the particulars of the universe, he was rewarded by a renewed involvement and reunion with the general. He was able to love all things, all nature, all people dispassionately, and to see in each the handiwork of God.

Non-attachment, however, was not, as Paul learned starting with discrimination between love and lust, the same as abstinence or total avoidance. One could partake but not desire. This distinction was the first step in loosening the bonds which enslave one to material objects, and represented a decentering or freeing of the mind so that other higher relationships could be envisaged. It was the difference between the man who picks the beautiful forest flower in order to possess it, and the one who admires it and lets it be for others to appreciate also. It was the start of a long process of unwrapping consciousness, which gradually and by stages allowed the little selfish ego to be replaced with something grander and more sublime. It was the first wiggle of the butterfly out of the chrysalis. When consciousness is encased in creaturehood, Paul found, it is hard not to be about the business of the creature.

The sensation of pricking in his hands and feet, and a curious heat in his lower back, with other more mental signs, signified to Paul that he was becoming ready to heal. His first actual experience, however, came about in a curious manner. Paul was eating in a rather ordinary restaurant. A somewhat nondescript waitress was struggling with a large tray. It was obvious from her flinching gesture that she was in pain. Something inside Paul said, "Help her." though she was turned away from him and too far away to touch, he instinctively held out his hand.

He was surprised when she turned around and exclaimed: "What did you do to me?"

"Is it better?" asked Paul.

"Yes," she replied, "but what did you do and how did you do it?"

"I don't know," confessed Paul, puzzled but happy.

This experience with the waitress was the first intimation Paul had that he could actually heal others. He then tried out his power on a few friends. Often it worked best with those of the opposite sex for whom he felt genuine love and sympathy, and he began to realize that this power was carried on emotions of love and compassion. One could not really heal others unless one loved and cared for them in a compassionate manner, non-judgemental and forgiving. The healing power came and went of its own accord, and of course, there were some whom he could not heal at all.

Paul began to realize that healing comes out of non-attachment; and as he continued to work, he discovered that in practice attachment to things mortal comes down to the nuances of the possessive pronoun "mine." First "mine" must lose its exclusivity: money is no more mine than is the sun; possessions are no more mine than the air we breathe. Later on, as the transformation passes from the possessive to the nominative, the character of I changes so that I is less a personal referent than merely the subjective awareness of the action. This understanding was the reason why many of the saints used the third person in speaking of themselves.

Paul had another notable healing experience, this time at a swimming pool. On getting out, he saw a vacant chair beside a middle-aged but attractive woman who was rubbing the calf of her leg. Always friendly, Paul sat down besire her and asked what was the matter. She indicated that it was a charley-horse. He asked if he could help and again on impulse began to rub her foot and toes. Surprisingly the spasm and pain immediately relaxed, and she thanked him and went to her room. The next day they were also at the pool, and the woman spoke first.

"What did you do to me yesterday?" she asked, wonderingly.

"Just helped you a bit," Paul replied, non-commitally.

"But the funny thing is, not only is my charley-horse gone, but a knee problem which I have had for some time is much better."

Paul's earlier realization that under some circumstance he could actually heal people was now further confirmed. He did not like to speak of the power in these terms; in fact he did not like to speak about it at all. Thereafter in a long series of experiences, — some successes, some partial successes, and some failures, Paul began to understand the dimensions and limits of this new gift. When he was able and about to heal, he would often feel somatic sensations of heat. Women were generally better subjects than men for him. He had to care for them personally, but without lust: as healer, he could not be indifferent, he must be compassionate. The energy flowed better when Paul was able to put his hands directly on the affected flesh, but this sort of intimate contact always held the danger in the case of young and pretty females that sexual excitation might arise in his heart, and this immediately "switched" the energy from healing to a lower outlet. The healing of functional pain such as headaches or backaches seemed easiest.

Healing also came easier to a patient, if the patient relaxed, believed in his power, or did something in the way of activity at the time of healing.

Paul began to notice what he called "a leveling-out of appetite." Previously he had looked forward with graduated anticipation to the compelling satisfaction of various foods, especially deserts and ice cream; in a similar manner he would anticipate with alluring fantasy the sexual satisfaction which successful lovemaking with some desirable woman would afford him. Life had been a series of events graded on a scale of pleasure or pain. Now however, two developments were apparent. First there was a lessening of all anticipations of the flesh, and a more detached attitude when they occurred. They were enjoyed or endured with equinaminity. They were not longed for; he had become less attached to them. Secondly, in place of these pleasures and glamours there arose a more steady but lower level satisfaction in the going-well of all things human, especially human interactions. It was as if one had acquired responsibilities for seeing that the flow of events went off smoothly, and one was pleased and somehow comforted that they did, for it seemed an omen of control over the environment, as though nature were obediently responding to the co-design of his consciousness with that of some cosmic order. Thus a walk in the park, a boat trip on a languid lagoon, a peaceful day, a successful meeting, a friendly luncheon, and general order in its proper place gave him some inner and pervasive satisfaction. The only "high spots" in his affect were provided for by breakthroughs of creativity in writing, and in dramatic success in healing others.

But along with these changes, there was another, curiously enough in the opposite direction. Paul's perception of nature somehow grew more acute. Blake had first noticed it in his famous statement, "the doors of perception were cleansed." Almost a universal experience of those privileged to have a theophany, somehow all of nature seemed brighter and more drenched with an ultraviolet light. It was as if some of the pristine iridescence of that first rapture had returned to remind him of its continuance. The sun seemed to shine with greater brilliance; the waves reflected a strange new light; it was as if higher octaves of the spectrum were about to be revealed to his eyes. Especially when he went out in the morning the grace and beauty of all nature sometimes overwhelmed him, and he felt like falling down on his knees and thanking God for the matchless bounty which had been afforded him. This delight in nature, in earth, sky and sea, never seemed to leave him.

Along with this development, there was an aural one to match. It consisted chiefly in the apprehension of an inner music, faint and fairy-like, sort of a singing in his heart. These sounds were impossible to describe or notate.

He also found himself taking pleasure in little things, — in the contemplation of a peaceful reach of water, or a dandelion, or a bird on the wing. The cosmic spirit seemed to say within him: "These are all myriad manifestations of my glory."

It is not surprising that a final grace was afforded him, — a continual inner stream of merriment which sprang from no perceptible cause but seemed to bubble forth like a spring of cold clear water. He found himself humming to it, and his smiles and good nature became apparent to all his friends and acquaintances.

What will Paul become — a healer, a hermit, a guru, a saint? It is too early to tell, since his life is ongoing. But perhaps in that lies the answer: the process is itself the goal; it is not self-actualization he seeks; it is rather self-actualizing.

4 — PAUL

[1] The famous vision of Dante as quoted by Underhill (1911:287).
[2] From Th. Traherne *"Centuries of Meditations."*

CHAPTER 5
Anne

It is not generally appreciated that there live among us quiet, "closet" mystics, who have experiences others would call weird, but to them are natural, who eat and drink, marry, beget, and bear children like the rest of us, but whose whole life seems shot through with visionary experience. Such a person is the woman I will call Anne. Pretty and intelligent, she is happily married to an adoring husband and has brought up a family of four children.

I was able to get an interview with Anne, which I report as a matter of record. I found her to be an amiable, healthy and generously endowed housewife who seemed in no way abnormal, but rather as well immersed in things material as any of the merry wives of Windsor. Nevertheless, there was something unique about her — something sparkling and refreshing, as if her spirit was constantly being replenished from some interior and secret source.

Amid all this mundane living, in fact attached to it in the most intimate manner, is a whole range of mystic experience. Since Anne is an earth mother, much of it is connected with love and child bearing. I have secured permission to reprint selected passages from her diary bearing on these matters. And have also included some conversations we had on her experiences.

"When did this sort of thing start with you?" I began.

"Ever since I can remember. I've always had interior experiences which I gradually learned others called "strange" but which for me seemed absolutely natural. When I was a child I could see the colors around people, and these colors (or auras, as I learned they were called) would tell me much about the state of health or the level of goodness in a particular individual. I could also often see fuzzy little flitting creatures, something like bees or hummingbirds that attended flowers, and wondered why others could not follow their flight. As I grew up, I learned that neither these friends nor these abilities of mine were understood or appreciated by others, and so I gradually left them off at adolescence.

"However, I continue to have sightings of these realms on occasion. Some would call them visions, others hallucinations or dreams, but to me they have a vivid reality that is more certain than ordinary existence. They often seem triggered by certain kinds of events and places. Of these, water, mountains, childbirth, or indeed any other event which arouses strong emotions are common triggers. So unusual did these scenes appear to me that I used to keep a special diary to record them. Here is one which happened when I was about eighteen. I had just gone to my uncle's farm in the country and had climbed up to my favorite belvedere, a rocky ledge surmounting a ridge behind the farm where one could look out on a distant vista of mountains.

"'I seated myself on a stone, and suddenly the Thing happened: I was absorbed in *suchness*. It cannot be correctly described in words, as everybody knows. If not taken literally the Bible phrase: 'I saw the Heavens open' seems as good as any. Something dazzling happened to the world: It became purer and more jewel-like. I remember whispering to myself in awe and rapture: 'So this is what it's like in Heaven.' Soon the wonder faded, and I was left alone again with only earthly beauty. But I was filled with great gladness for I had seen the far distances."[1]

"Did this sort of thing scare you?" I asked.

"Oh no," she replied. "I considered it natural, though it generally has some unusual setting. Here's an example:"

[2]"I was weekending in the country. Upon hearing the good news about the end of hostilities, with great thankfulness in my heart I went out onto the verandah and looked across at the darkening hills. It was a beautiful moonless evening and all the stars were out in their glory. Suddenly it seemed my soul opened up to them, out as it were into the Infinite, and there was a merging together of the two worlds, those of outer space and of inner concern. It was the deep calling unto the deep — the deep that my own struggle had opened up within, being answered by the unfathomable deep without, reaching to and beyond the stars. I stood alone with Him who had made me. I did not seek Him but felt the perfect union of my spirit with His. Ordinary senses of things around me faded, and for one moment nothing but ineffable joy and exaltation remained. It is, of course, impossible fully to describe such an experience. It was like the effect of some great orchestra when all the separate notes and choirs have melted into one swelling harmony that leaves the listener conscious of nothing save that his soul is being lifted upwards, bursting with its lofty emotion. The perfect stillness of the night was surpassed by an even more solemn silence. For the darkness held a Presence that was more felt because it was not seen. I could not anymore have doubted that He was there than that I was. My highest faith in God was then born in me. I have stood since on the mound of vision and felt the Eternal around me. But

never since has there come quite the same stirring of the heart and the feeling of standing face to face with God Himself."[2]

"Have you had many of these 'nature' experiences?" I asked.

"Oh yes, a good many. Let me read several others from my diary." [3]"I was alone in a forest preserve and came by accident to a beautiful waterfall which culminated in a small lake. Suddenly the scene seemed to shift — I never could decide how — and the rocks behind the waterfall appeared to move with the flowing water. All at once I experienced a feeling of being raised above myself. I felt the presence of God amid this beauty, as if His goodness and power were penetrating me altogether. The emotion was so violent that I could not stand. I sat down on a large stone, and my eyes brimmed with tears. For the walls between the visible and the invisible had parted, and the Eternal seemed to break through into my world. I saw no flood of light and heard no voice, but I felt the presence of a higher order of reality. I became conscious of an unutterable stillness, and every object about me seemed bathed in a soft ethereal light."[3]

"What use do you make of such experiences?" I questioned.

"It's no use asking what good is a grace," she laughingly replied. "It's just a favor that God grants to some of us. It is meant to please us, like giving candy to a child." "It fills one's heart with peace and gladness, like this one.

[4]It happenend this morning that I was out walking in the woods and had arrived at a favorite clearing where the pines and hemlocks formed a perfect backdrop for a tableau. I sat down to meditate on this beautiful natural sight. All at once I saw that I was surrounded by a troop of heavenly spirits. They were transparent and radiant, every one, and I had communication in the mind with the first among them, having asked in my heart of this prince of the sky how God dwelt in my soul. The angel replied, 'Do but fix your eyes joyously upon yourself, and watch how God plays the game of love within your loving soul.'

Looking quickly at myself, I saw that my body in the region of my heart was pure and transparent like crystal, and Saint Sophia, the angel of Divine Wisdom, was enthroned peacefully therein; she was radiant and fair to look upon, being exceedingly comely, and holding a ring in her hand on which was a diamond. . .

Then my heart was filled with peace and gladness, and I beheld the angelic chorus in song of praise to God the Father."[4]

[5]"On another occasion when I had come to the same cherished spot to meditate I had had a vision of a different kind. I can only call it intellectual, for I felt myself encased in God, and His angels were all around me though I saw and heard nothing out of the ordinary. Yet there was a sweet Presence everywhere; and, I felt, in a way much more exalted

than was customary for me, that I seemed to be in the midst of the Trinity and enjoyed without interruption the blessing of so being placed. And thus to be totally absorbed in God filled me with greatest delight. And feeling myself to be in this beatitude and experiencing this great and unspeakable delight, which was more than any I had had before, such ineffable thoughts took place in my soul that neither saint not angel could explain. And though I saw and understood then those Divine operations and that unfathomable abyss which no creature however wise can comprehend, all that I can say about it now seems so far from the true case as to be virtual blasphemy."[5]

"Today I went to my favorite grove to meditate. But before I could do so, as I sat down on a rock it seemed as though a curtain were drawn away across the landscape and a new universe became visible. At first there were little flecks and stars blurring my vision, and I seemed to hear a rushing sound. Then all was still and I heard as if at a distance the low and undistinguishable murmur of men talking at some remove from me. I tried to listen more intently but could not make out any words. Then it seemed as though they came nearer but became invisible, for I felt presences around me in the grove and heard soft sweet music as if played on a lyre. My heart overflowed with an unusual peace, and as I looked at the flora, each plant seemed to vibrate with life, and I was part of that teeming life. I felt a wonderful kinship with all the universe, as if I had come at last to realize my perfect part and participation in it. It was so perfect, complete and beautiful that my emotions overflowed, and I started to cry with the goodness and wonder of it. The presences then departed slowly, but I felt cleansed and hallowed by this experience, as if I had been left a blessing. I fell to my knees and thanked God for His love and mercy to me."

"You can see that these are unexpected blessings." She added at the end of her story.

"Do you often share these experiences with others?" I asked her after hearing those detailed above.

"I am very selective in this," she replied, "as I have found out that most people regard one as slightly crazy and really do not want to hear about such matters. I have shared some of them with my husband and one other older friend, but that is all."

"Is it difficult or easy for you to have these visions?"

"It is very easy for me to have these experiences, which are of relative frequency. They are generally occasioned by the sight of sudden beauty of a natural kind, under conditions when I am relaxed and at peace. Sudden good news, which brings a relaxation in tension, or some sense of psychic relief will also bring on these spells."

"Your letter told me that many of your experiences were connected with love and marriage. Could we hear some of these?" I interposed.

"When I first became interested in boys and love-making, it was too new and exciting for me to think much of its mystical aspects. But later as I became more accustomed to it, and had experienced my first orgasms, I became aware that the total absorption in another person, so that the two of us became one, at least for a little while had some very significant overtones. It would seem to me that we were locked in bliss, and I would experience a sense of such deep contentment and union, that I would hardly be aware of my own personality as distinct from his. There was a kind of primordial perfection in this conjugal embrace, an original connectedness which restored a dissevered world to its primitive order and completeness."

"I cannot tell you how it is for others, but when the man I love enters me, all at once I am suffused with an exquisite wholeness; it is more than physical, it is some escape into a primordial completeness. I do not need an orgasm to validate that experience for me. As I lie enfolded in him, and he in me, we are one, whole, beyond time and space, almost beyond personality. There is content, security and rest that I cannot begin to describe in words. I should die if I should continue very long in that state, and for me the orgasm is the release from this overwhelming bliss back into mortality."

"Then you see sexual love as a virtual mystic experience?" I asked.

"Yes," Anne replied, "it is often that way for me. I see no difference in the various kinds of love; somehow they all blend together. Here is an example of that."

"A somewhat curious experience occasionally occurs when my husband and I are making love. I prefer him in the superior position with my legs embracing his. After ardent mutual lovemaking, we often have simultaneous orgasms of a convulsive nature, during which I become aware of a peculiar phenomenon. I ask him to remain for a while still inside of me while all his precious fluid drains into my womb. While this takes place, it would sometimes seems that we are enveloped in a cloudy film of some fiery substance which first appears thick and red, but gradually thins to a lighter pink, and is finally extinguished with the momentary appearance of little twinkling stars. The film at the start seems so thick and opaque as to be inpenetrable, but then it becomes translucent and then like a colored mist until the pink plasma vanishes in little pinpricks of light. I cannot adequately explain the extraordinary sense of rest, comfort and peace which accompanies this phenomenon. When I finally release my husband from this nuptial embrace, he is nearly asleep, and evidently has not seen anything, so whatever it may be, is apparently a private perception."

"But do you think that this passion is compatible with Divine love?" I queried.

"Oh yes," she replied. "I sometimes think that God is passonate in his love for humankind. Only His passion vastly exceeds ours in that it is purer and nobler. But the nearest that we can come to its fervor is the intensity that we have in our overwhelming love for our lover which we have at the time of sexual union. One is then willing to lose oneself absolutely, if need be to sacrifice all for this love — to give the all for the all. It is comforting to me to feel that God has this passion for us and that all we need to do is to return it to Him."

"And do you have similar experiences connected with childbirth?" I asked.

"Oh yes, I had visions with all four of my children's births. Here they are."

[6]"As they gave me anesthesia for the delivery of my first baby, I closed my eyes and watched a silver glow, which whirled itself into a circle with a central focus brighter than the rest. The circle became a tunnel of light still whirling at the edges, opening from myself to some distant sun. Smoothly and swiftly I as borne through this silver tunnel; and as I went, the light gently turned from silver to gold. There was an impression of drawing strength from a limitless sea of power and a sense of deepening peace. The light grew brighter, but not dazzling nor alarming, and I finally came to a point where time and motion ceased, and I was absorbed in the light of the universe. This Reality glowed like fire with the knowledge of itself; and I, without ceasing to be myself, merged like a drop of mercury with the Whole, yet still somehow separated. Then I realized that the peace which passeth understanding and the pulsating energy of creation are one in the center where all opposites are reconciled. I was at utter peace within and without. Slowly I drifted back to consciousness as my baby was laid on my belly."[6]

"When I was delivering my second child they gave me something — I do not know to this day what it was — but it produced a dreamy fantasy state, which seemed absolutely real and very beautiful. I was in a lovely place where everything in the landscape had a shining, gem-like quality — a kind of rainbow translucence. This many-hued aura surrounded everything with an egg-shaped nebulous covering, consisting of transparent and ever-changing colors. Everything seemed in vibration, in harmony, as if singing a celestial chorus in color. Furthermore, there was a misty gemlike quality to the very sticks and stones, as if everything had a shining interior, which I was now privileged to see for the first time."

"But the shining was not fire; it was more like the cold rainbow rays emitted by a crystal of ice when irradiated by the sun. And each lumination had a peculiar glow, as if it conveyed not only a particular hue on the visible octave but also its overtones in the ultra violet. These latter seemed to pierce my brain and register immediately on my mind with some compelling higher urgency and energy. It was as if the light were alive, holy, imperious, and absolute. I felt awed by the sight."

'I seemed to enter a glass solarium, or similar structure, which let in a great quantity of light from the sun but refracted it in such a curious fashion that I could perceive all colors of the rainbow at once. Within this edifice was a fabulous treasury of precious jewels larger and more beautiful than any I had ever seen. They were also set and displayed so as to show a maximum amount of fire and radiance, which was sometimes so intense as to be painful to my eyes. There were diamonds of all sizes and shapes, pearls, jaspers, onyx, opal, amethyst, carnelians, sapphire, emeralds and beryl, to name but a few."

"But the surprising thing was how these gems sparkled and glistened in the light. It seemed as if the whole were irradiated with such brilliances that their luminosity spread forth in every direction with an almost blinding light. The display was something like a thousand arc lights playing hither and yon, only so many that night, or whatever it was, was transformed into a daylight brighter than the sun."

"Fiery rays played everywhere, and the stones seemed to burn with exotic brilliance and effulgence. Moreover it seemed as though this arcana of treasure had discovered other and more brilliant colors never before brought to mind, or else I was enabled to see higher octaves of the spectrum and to understand the fullness of light in all its luminosity, much as if my vision had widened and the doors of perception had been scrubbed clean to reveal in all its splendid wonder the treasures of heaven. I wandered from marvel to marvel, from one iridescent jewel to another, brighter, larger with more sparkle. I was amazed beyond rational comparison, drunk with this sensory overload, and sated with the consequent euphoria it produced. Eventually, my eyes began to dazzle, and I could only perceive a dreamy, phosphorescent, multicolored mist. Then I lapsed into a deep sleep."

"Some considerable time later, when all this wondrous glory had faded, I was brought to myself by a nurse gently awakening me, 'Here is your baby,' she said, 'you had a very easy time of it.' "

"With my third child there were some complications, and I was thoroughly put to sleep. I felt myself whirling in a revolving tunnel, coming out at last to face a blinding light. My individuality seemed to dissolve before it, melting into a kind of omniscient consciousness."

[7]"An inner and esoteric meaning began to come to me from all the visible universe; I now became lost and absorbed in the being or existence of all life and, losing thus my separateness of being came near to seem like a part of the Whole. I felt on the verge of a life unknown, on the margin of powers, which, once grasped, could give all men an immense breadth of existence. I experienced a new kind of radiance, a

flooding of my being with new light, which transfigured the twilight world in which I had formerly lived. It was rare and untellable. It was living and intense; it was an infused brightness, a light which knows no darkness."[7]

"I did not want to leave this wondrous realm, but voices kept calling me back to mortality. At length I was slowly detached from this something and floated back to the hospital room, slowly coming to with nurses and doctors standing around me. 'Is the baby all right?' I asked. 'Yes, it is,' someone said. 'That's fine,' I replied, and then I dropped off to sleep."

"My fourth and last child was an easy birth. When they gve me something, I suddenly found my self in the new Jerusalem. [8]Certainly Adam in Paradise had not more sweet and curious apprehension of the world than I. All appeared new and strange at first, inexpressibly rare and delightful . . . All things were spotless and pure and glorious. I knew not that there were any sins. I dreamed not of poverty or vice. Everything was at rest, free and immortal. All time was eternity. Is it not strange that an infant should be heir to the whole world and see those mysteries which the books of the learned never unfold?"

"The corn was orient and immortal wheat which never should be reaped, nor was ever sown. I thought it had stood from everlasting to everlasting. The dust and stones of the street were as precious as gold. The green trees, when I saw them first through the gates, transported and ravished me. What reverend creatures did the aged seem! And the young men, glittering and sparkling angels; and maids, strange seraphic pieces of life and beauty; boys and girls, tumbling in the streets and playing, were moving jewels. I knew not that they were ever born to should die. But all things abided eternally as they were in their proper places. Eternity was manifest in the light of day, and something infinite behind everyhting appeared. The city seemed to stand in Eden or be build in Heaven."[8]

"I cannot descirbe with what peace I returned to consciousness. I knew the baby would be perfect and it was. I felt as if I had been privileged to look in on heaven."

"You report a lot of these visions. How often would you say that you have them?" I asked.

"Not very often. They usually come under a condition of relaxation from a particular stress circumstance. I have sometimes gone for several months without having one; but again, I have had them as often as once a week," she replied.

"Can you induce them at will?"

"No, they come of their own accord. I visualize them as nothing unusual, but as the permanent condition in another realm which I can only get into in an altered state of consciousness. For me that realm is real, like a magic garden; but I can enter it only under very favorable conditions."

"What are the conditions?" I persisted.

"Well, it's a little like the mechanics of a lucid dream, I visualize that this reality, the one we call 'real' is as Hesse said, a 'magic threatre' where in fact everything is a dream. Omar Khayyam called it a 'magic lantern show.' I see this phantasmagoria, which we call life, as a waking dream. Occasionally some of us arouse from this dream to see another reality, like Plato's man in the cave who goes outside and sees the sun. He realizes that outside the cave is the real world, and what he and others have watched on the wall are merely shadow figures. So it is with me."

"Do you have any techniques to help you visualize that realm?" I queried.

"Well, it is a matter of getting one's consciousness to awake in that state. And this starts by calming the sensory input and the internal chatter. Meditation is best for this, for it shuts down the senses when one closes one's eyes, and the mantra tends to shut off the stream-of-consciousness chatter that would otherwise go on interminably."

"Do you have any unusual effects from this practice?"

"Well sometimes I have what psychologiests call auditory or visual hallucinations. I will hear the low voices of men talking at a distance, though I cannot make out the words, or I will see flashes and specks before my eyes. Often times I am awakened in the morning by what seems to be a telephone bell, but is really only in my mind. I regard these as mere epiphenomena. When I am about to have a vision, I have a kind of premonition due to the way things still down; and my mind seems unusually filled with peace. Then just before the vision, it seems like there is some change in the sky. If you look at the color of the sky above and below a rainbow, that is the kind of change I am talking about."

"Do you literally see your visions occupying physical space?" I asked.

With laughter in her eyes, and a smile she couldn't hold back, she replied, "That's the kind of question you get with a misperceived premise. the vision is an appearance of reality in another space; it is real in that real realm, though it is an apparition in our dream realm. It can no more be explained using the premise of our realm than the sun can be explained by looking at the shadows on Plato's wall."

"But if the vision is an apparition in our realm, with what sensory apparatus do you perceive it?"

"I perceive it in the mind's eye — internally, if you will. This is another question which is based on a false premise, so really has no good answer. I believe the mind has powers we know not of, and this ability to intuit reality internally is one of them."

"Are your visions, if I may call them that, religiously or sectarian oriented? Have they changed your philosophy or beliefs?" I questioned in conclusion.

"They are not oriented toward any sect. Sometimes they are of religious aspects, and sometimes natural. Sometimes I see a Cosmic Presence, and sometimes I only feel it. I look upon nature as the garments of God, so for me, to see Him with His beautiful clothes is as good as seeing Him in other ways. No one can have such visions without feeling that the universe is orderly and good and that there is on-going life after death, though not necessarily in our individualistic and selfish forms. But the visions leave me with a sense of being cleansed and purified and with a general optimism for both my own future and the future of mankind as well."

★ ★ ★

Is Anne a saint? She would be the last so to claim. She does not even go to church regularly. She obviously enjoys married love with her husband and is a hearty eater and a proficient square dancer — all activities not in keeping with our usual picture of a saintly life. But perhaps we have Medieval ideas about Saints colored by the customs of those times. Or perhaps Anne was a saint in a past life, and is "on furlough" enjoying the gratifications of this one. Perhaps there are no answers to this question; perhaps it is another with a poor premise. But one thing is sure: Anne is an unusual person, a healthy, useful, joyful extrovert who, with her family and friends and in her own way, is brightening up life for those lucky enough to know and love her.

For notes to this chapter see page 141.

CHAPTER 6
Marie

The woman whom I will call "Marie" came to my attention in several ways almost simultaneously. She was pointed out to me by a junior staffer as "an odd character, not interested in a degree, but only in self-actualization itself." She received a high score on the self-actualizing scale of the *Northridge Development Scale,* which I myself had produced for screening guidance candidates in the Department. Finally, she came to see me to inquire what factors I had in mind in devising the scale and what books I could recommend that she read in order to help her attain self-actualization more quickly and easily. Since all three of these behaviors were rather unusual, I decided that I ought to look into the matter more closely, as I was ultimately responsible. Our first interview proved to be somewhat of a shocker.

But first let me introduce myself. For many years I was a professor of educational psychology in a California State University. As such, my major responsibilities were to guide graduate students in the Guidance master's candidates field. As our department was humanistically oriented and enjoyed a wide reputation, we attracted a great many students who wished to avoid the "rat-oriented" reductionist views of some of my more positivistic colleagues elsewhere. We had so many candidates, in fact, that we had to do some screening. Since we were interested in candidates with a high degree of mental health, I had devised the *Northridge* with its scale of self-actualizing aspects, modeled somewhat after the Shostrom POI. This was routinely given to all entering candidates.

Marie appeared as a stylish and attractive woman in her late forties, married with nearly grown children and with an unusual air. She was obviously in no financial difficulties, and was, like many other women of her age, involved in a consciousness-raising attempt after her maternal functions were over. But this was consciousness-raising with a vengeance. For Marie exuded an upper-class patrician air which was charming without being the least offensive or patronizing. She appeared like some kind of disenfranchised royalty, too noble for sex appeal, though she would otherwise have been a very desirable woman, — and too ethereal for the coarser aspects of the world. She expressed kindness, confidence, trust and indeed all the virtues, but there was something strange about her nevertheless. Imagine the daughter of a distant, but noble branch of your family, a cross between the innocence of *Alice in Wonderland* and the resourcefulness of *Mary Poppins* — something like a favorite older cousin, who has just been named a duchess, and you will have something of the aura of reverence and affection which Marie inspired on sight. She was guileless and I am convinced absolutely truthful to the extent that she said only what she believed. This is important as you shall soon see.

If Marie's appearance was somewhat unusual, her story was even more spectacular. I have pieced it together from a number of talks with Marie, for she was very reticent about telling it for obvious reasons. Here it is in a nutshell.

As a young girl from an upper-middle class family, and just out of college, she married after a real love affair a strong, ambitious and handsome man, by whom she had had three children, now grown up. He was a mining engineer, and frequently away from home but they had a strong family life, nevertheless. When her children were in their early teens, he had unfortunately been killed in a mining accident. She quickly dried her tears, however, and soon married a very wealthy man, retired and considerably older, and they had traveled extensively. She enjoyed this comfortable life but it was suddenly brought to a close by his untimely death from a heart attack. Still attractive, although in her forties, she had married shortly after a brilliant pianist several years her junior.

This marriage was unlike the others. For one thing, with a brilliant career in the ascendant, her husband was frequently away on long professional tours. He had refused to touch a penny of her money and thus needed to support himself by constantly giving recitals in the U.S. and Europe. He was attentive and nurturing to her during the times when he was at home and she enjoyed this companionship very much. He was also attuned to her strong interests in art and music and seemed to have a higher spiritual quality than her first two husbands. He was a tee-totaler and a vegetarian and soon after marriage had asked her if they could give up sexual contact, since it seemed to him to interfere with his performance capacity at the piano. She was entranced with his high level of development, which was something she had looked for in a man, but never found, and readily agreed to all that he requested.

At this point I raised an obvious question. "If you had the means, and enjoyed travel, why did you not accompany your husband on his tours?"

Without a moment's hesitation, she replied, "For several reasons: First, he felt that he could not do me justice when he was so busy, and I would have tired of one-night stands and the rigors of profesional tours. Secondly, someone was really needed to take care of financial matters at home and to oversee the children's college educations. And, finally, we were both rather serious-minded people and he felt that I should employ this time in graduate study."

"What kind of study?" I asked.

"This kind," she immediately responded.

"To get a master's degree?" I asked.

"No just to help me understand self-actualization better, and to become more self-actualizing myself."

"Why would he want that?"

"So I would become more like him, and could perhaps follow him."

"I don't understand what you mean by 'follow'."

"So, I could follow in his footsteps, and go where he has gone."

"Where has he gone?"

"He has become translated. I don't know quite how to tell you this, but he has given up his mortal body, and has become a spirit."

"You mean he has died?"

"Oh, no! Let me explain it to you in detail. Sometime after our marriage when he felt full confidence in me, he revealed that he was a disciple of Annalee Skarin, the auther of *Ye Are Gods,* who believed literally in translation to another realm and had actually made the change herself."

"I can scarcely believe this."

"I assure you it is the truth. He told me that he had long followed the book's precepts and it had recently been revealed to him that he would soon be translated himself as Anne had been."

"You mean to say, he predicted his own d--- change?"

"Yes, and moreover he told me it would come in stages, so that he would be able to visit me and so comfort me at night in a vision and then later in dreams."

"Were you not confused and alarmed by this? Did you not think that he was having mental trouble?"

"Oh, there was no sign of that; he was as normal and loving as ever."

"Didn't you try to dissuade him or stop him?"

"How could I?; Obviously the experience was a culmination of something he had worked for; moreover it was ennobling and beautiful."

"When did all this happen?"

"Last spring on his annual trip to Europe. Before he went, he talked to me tenderly and seriously one night and told me that he felt something very important was about to happen, and that I was not to worry; he loved me and would never forget me. Someday, we would be together again."

"Then what happened?"

"He went on his tour. Sometime after I received a last letter from him, saying that he had been told he was about ready to make the change. One night shortly after this, I had a vivid dream in which he appeared to me and told me that that transistion was imminent and that I must not be disturbed or anxious for him. He also told me he still loved me, and would appear to me again."

"But surely, this disappearance would occasion some inquiry?"

"No, he said, that was taken care of; there would be no fuss."

"Then what happened?"

"One night, shortly after, when I was in bed, he appeared to me, whether in the flesh or a vision I do not know, and talked tenderly to me about personal matters, and his hope that I would be able to follow him in his translation."

"What did he want you to do?"

"Just what I am doing now. To enroll here. Because he said there was a humanistically-oriented faculty here, which would be receptive to my needs, and he particularly pointed out that you were here and that you would understand these matters."

Rather taken aback by this intuition I pressed further, "Did he then give you permission to tell me all these strange matters?"

"Oh yes, that is the only reason I am telling you."

"What else did he enjoin upon you?"

"Several rules: First careful reading of the book by Annalee Skarin, second, meditation daily, third, giving up liquor, red meat and sex, and, lastly, coming here to take graduate courses. He said if I followed these injunctions carefully, I myself would be translated and eventually rejoin him. I have taken an apartment near the university expressly for this purpose."

"You actually mean, you expect to be translated, yourself?"

"I don't think anyone at my stage of development can say that; I am following my husband's precepts in the hopes that that may happen, but even if it does not the work itself is ennobling."

I must say that this conversation left my mind reeling; I had the greatest difficulty in believing it, yet I felt obligated to keep an open mind. I tried on many subsequent occasions to shake Marie's story, but never succeeded. She regarded my doubt with amused tolerance, and even teased me about it. Her husband had told her not to tell others, because they would not believe her.

"Why did you then tell me?" I asked.

"I asked him for special permission to do so, and after he checked you he granted it, saying that you were ready for this kind of

60

enlightenment?"

"What do you mean, he 'checked' me?"

"He looks into your mind: Then he tells me what is there. For example you have been wondering about the Skarin book, — is there such a thing. He told me to give you my copy, since I am to have his."

She handed me the book *Ye Are Gods* which I hold in my hand as I write.

"Well, how do you get in touch with him?" I asked.

"Simple, I just think of the questions I want answered before going to sleep and either he will visit me at night, or he will put the answer into my mind next morning on waking."

"You mean to say I could carry on a conversation with your husband in this way?"

"Sure, just tell me what you want answered and next time I see you I'll have it. Often times he tells me what you want to know before you voice it."

I must say that I even carried on some kind of conversation with her husband in this round-about manner, and I was shaken by the uncanny accuracy of his responses. He knew I was writing a book on the general subject, that I had developed a test for self-actualization, and apparently that I would be supportive of Marie at this critical time in her life. I had, however, a duty not only to myself but to my colleagues and the university to subject this story of hers to the most rigorous testing I could. Before I could formulate a procedure, I had another meeting with Marie.

"He says I am to be very kind to you and patient in answering your doubts about this story," she informed me.

I must admit she hit the bullseye again for I was in the process of evolving and testing several hypotheses about Marie. The first was that she was psychotic and her story the result of some delusion. Fortunately I had the means at hand to give this possibility the most careful exploration. The test I had developed and used on guidance candidates, the *Northridge,* contains three negative check scales, any one of which would be tripped by a psychotic. There was no evidence of this whatever; according to the test, she was in excellent mental health. A careful inquiry among my colleagues as to her behavior in class revealed no abnormalities. My own talks with her confirmed her good mental health. Finally, psychotics do not do well on class tests and grades. Marie got A's. The worst that one could say about Marie from the standpoint of a psychological evaluation would be that her naive and Pollyannish outlook sometimes approached a mild mania but there never seemed to be a depressed period connected therewith. Instead she seemed to be nourished from some inner spring of strength and joy.

My second hypothesis, seemed much more plausible on the surface, because Marie was unusual in having a rich fantasy life and in seeing people and events as more ideal than they are. In a nutshell, it is that while normal Marie was given to fantasy, and after the death of two husbands she had fantasized marriage to a third, who did not actually exist. It is, of course, possible that she had fantasized marriage to an idealized image who was younger and possessed of something she valued, namely, musical talent. (To me the younger man was particularly telling in suggesting the idealized situation, since it would tend to preclude a third husband dying on her as had two already. I felt further reinforced in this idea, by the fact that she did not use her third husband's last name).

"How is it that you do not use your husband's surname?" I asked one day.

"Oh, he told me you would ask that," she replied, laughing. "But it is really very simple. After the death of my second husband, I resumed my first husband's name because of the children and the less need for explanations. Before marriage, my present husband and I had an agreement that I would not use his name, — which was really a professional one — for the same reason. He also said you were doubtful that I ever married him, so I have brought wedding pictures, and the names of witnesses to show you if you wish. It was on the beach of Kona, Hawaii."

She added other details of the nuptials, including the guests. Of course, all this could have been fabricated, but the verisimilitude of her answers and her childlike ingenuousness struck me as adding corroboration to her story.

There was another darker hypothesis, that of "the disappearing husband" one, which must be considered, for in many ways, mostly cynical, it was the most plausible explanation. I reasoned that one might suppose that a brilliant young pianist has sexual deviation problems, and is anxious to provide a cover for them. He meets a rich older naive woman, who can care for herself and family financially, and can provide a haven he can return to after his tours. Such a set-up might be very tempting. But as many people in similar circumstances have found out, normality palls and the young man wants out. How does he do it? The translation story constitutes a most ingenious solution. While it presents some difficulties, such as the temporary interruption of his career, it is one that cannot be totally disregarded. I was never able to give this hypothesis the thorough checking it deserved and I must leave it to you to decide if it is applicable.

I now come to an examination of the most startling aspect of this whole business: namely that what Marie told me was literally true. I know that the transcendental hypothesis may seem preposterous, but every hypothesis must be examined with rigor by a scholar who wishes to find the truth. To gain a purchase on this problem, one might formulate some leading questions: 1) Are there any discrepancies in Marie's story which could be shown to be false? 2) Does the Annalee Skarin book provide information about the procedure for translation? 3) What research information outside this book regarding translation is available? 4) Was Marie's behavior consistent with the teaching she purported to believe in?

First let me dispose of the matter of the book. *Ye Are Gods* by Annalee Skarin was published in 1952 by the Philosophical Library in New York. The book is Mormon-oriented, has 26 chapters of highly religious verbiage, and contains 342 pages. On unnumbered page vi there is an editor's note which says:

"Soon after publishing this, the first edition of this remarkable book the author, Annalee Skarin, according to affidavits in our files, underwent a physical change known as "translation" as did Enoch of Biblical days."

The copy of the book, which Marie left with me, has many underlined passages, which in some ways are the most persuasive of all. For they show that somebody had studied the Skarin book with great diligence and attention. It was interesting to me that none of the underlined passages referred specifically to Mormon doctrines nor to the Christian trinity, though there was plenty of that in the book itself. Instead, the thought of meditation and emotion as producing healing vibrations is in line with many other esoteric teachings. Whoever underlined that book was certainly not psychotic nor unscrupulous but in full possession of cognitive faculties and obviously interested in self actualization.

And now to answer the questions earlier raised: 1) There were no discrepancies in Marie's story, 2) The Skarin book did provide information, 3) There is available research on translation outside the Skarin book, and 4) Marie's behavior was consistent with the teaching she purported to believe in. If you wish to explore additional documentation of these unusual facts you will find the results of my further researches in the notes.

Piecing together what the book said, especially in the underlined passages and some hints Marie gave, it seems that these people believed that through meditation, prayer, and ascetic living, one begins to set up a sort of vibration in the mind. This vibration, as it becomes more complete, begins to resonate with the cosmic. When this resonance is perfected, whatever is true on the cosmic plane also becomes true on the personal. Then it becomes possible to transcend mortality, for the body disappears in a flash of cosmic light. I stress that this is mere speculation on my part, since I do not pretend to understand fully the phenomenon.

I have dwelt on the transcendental hypothesis, because it raises some startling issues, going far beyond the principals in the case. I have presented the evidence as fairly as I know how. I draw no conclusion; that is reserved for you to decide. I will say that this incident is one of the most baffling and intriguing that has ever come to my attention during my entire educational career.

And what of Marie? That too is open-ended. I retired in the year that Marie was in residence, and went to New Zealand to teach and lecture for a short term. When I returned, I found Marie had dropped out of the program and efforts to reach her were unavailing. The telephone was disconnected; she had apparently moved; I had neglected to get the names and addresses of her children and no further trace of her was possible. We shall apparently never know whether or not she was successful in forming "a complete vibration" or whether her reach exceeded her grasp. But I must applaud a life filled with bold and noble purpose.

For notes to this chapter see page 143.

CHAPTER 7
Glen

Glen Mercer was born in a fashionable section of Murray Hill, New York City, just after the turn of the century. His father was an enterprising soft goods salesman who traveled in New Jersey and New England. His mother was the youngest and most rebellious daughter from an in-grown family of prosperous Maine farmers. She had met his father during one of the latter's travels through New England and they had eloped, much to the condemnation of the rest of the family, which consisted of three older sisters and two consumptive brothers, both of whom had died in adolescence. Glen's grandfather was a stern New Englander, who unconsciously felt that no-one should marry, and the three elder sisters never did.

The birth of their first (and only) grandson did a great deal to soften the feelings of the old man toward his errant daughter and son-in-law, and from the time Glen could remember he recalled lazy summers spent on the Maine farm, jumping in the hay mows, watching the milking of the cows, riding on the teeming hay wagons while sweating hired hands pushed up the bundles for packing. There were strawberries and blueberries and raspberries to pick and eat, and fishing excursions battling the flies with his grandfather to see if the Dolly Vardens were rising that afternoon. There were the piping hot country suppers, complete with fresh vegetables, cakes and pies. There was the pantry with its indescribably sweet, pungent smell which reminded one of Christmas cookies. There was the train whistle to lull one to sleep during the long summer twilights while the elders sat on the porch, and there was the whirring of the cream separator to wake one gently in the morning. Glen would peep out of his tiny attic room under the eaves, put on his robe, and run down the steep stairs to see the last of the cream and skim milk come out and to watch his aunts stoke the wood fire in the kitchen by the stove.

But "your old-maid Aunts" as his father called them, were Glen's chief delight. They were all much older than his mother and somehow impregnably virgin. The eldest were Nettie and Nellie who were identical twins. This likeness, however, did not prevent them from quarrelling gently during most of their waking hours. There was even a family couplet about their behavior:

Says Nettie to Nellie: You're quite an old cheese.
I'll ask your advice then do as I please.

Despite this act they were very close to each other and would resent and attack anyone who got between them or who even tried to make peace. Of the two, Nellie was slightly the more intellectual and peppery; and Nettie, slightly the more emotional and kindly. Nellie had gone for a while to the Gorham seminary, but she missed Nettie, who didn't choose to go, and so came home. This was the only outside-the-family experience they had ever had. Needless to say, they had been well educated in domestic duties by their mother and were accomplished cooks and seamstresses, each arguing with the other as to the best way to cook a capon or stitch a seam. Nellie, who had more pretense to culture, would read a lot, occasionally quote a Latin epigram, and wear a lavender choker around her neck to keep her head up and to show that she was somewhat more than a mere country girl, while Nettie would make fun of her by mimicking her actions. They had been to Portland twice to the fair, and once had ridden on the cars to Bridgeton and Poland Spring, on the pleas that the waters might be good for their brother; but Grampa Stone had soon detected carnal attractions along the way and at the spa and had forbidden any further such adventures. Full of energy and debarred from many pursuits normal for their age and sex, Nettie and Nellie turned to the church where their work with the Sunday School and the Missionary society, not to mention the choir and the ladies aid, was exemplary. Had there been only one of them, she would probably have become Sunday School Superintendent, but as there were two, it would have been impossible to give the job to either. So, a weak-chinned piano tuner was given the title though the real work was done by the sisters. Naturally, since it was one avenue of affection that was not proscribed, their love became focused on their young nephew.

Thoroughly cowed and subdued by the age and energies of these two was their much younger sister Bessie, who, also consumptive and sickly, presented the natural target of all weak and defenseless people. After the deaths of her two older brothers, Bessie was expected to die daily. This moribund posture protected her from the stricture of her father and the incessant energies of her sisters; she simply retired to her room and awaited the call, which, of course, never came. Because, perhaps, she had been so often abjured to prepare her soul for the hereafter, she was of very forgiving and kind nature, her favorite gesture being to wring her hands and murmur, "Poor Glen, what are we coming to?" Consequently, of all his Aunts she was his favorite.

Grandmother Berenthia Stone was an invalid, who, because of a previous stroke, was confined to a wheel chair. Fortunately none of her senses nor her speech nor intellect was involved, so that she remained while chair-bound the dominating female figure of the Maine farmhouse. She had been an accomplished musician on the organ and even gave infrequent music lessons to neighbor girls. She also had "second sight", perhaps a legacy from Scotch forebears, and sometimes saw and talked with "spirits," being an ardent believer in the hereafter and the ability of those there to walk the earth again. Grandma's sitting room was a dark, perfumed parlor where one was rarely allowed except on Sundays when the family gathered there to sing hymns after Sunday dinner of chicken fried as only the girls could do it. The only other occasion was family prayers, which were conducted by Grandfather on his knees directly before supper. Only Grandma was excused from kneeling, while the rest of the family gathered around her wheel-chair as the old man intoned a psalm, (generally the first), followed by family petitions for health and for the moral reform of anyone who had transgressed during the last twenty-four hours and followed by his unvarying peroration delivered in a falsetto Maine twang with heavy nasal overtones:

"Tarn ye, Tarn ye, for the end of sinners is hellfire and damnation eternal!"

Grandma had been known to object that such words of "hellfire" and "damnation" were not appropriate in her parlor, but Grandfather would always insist that they were in the Bible and hence quite worthy when used sincerely on such an occasion.

Because it was such a proscribed precinct, Grandma's sitting room was of peculiar interest to Glen. To begin with, there was the stereoscope, cards of two similar pictures, which when you looked through the apparatus at them seemed three-dimensional. Niagara Falls really came to life under this treatment, and so did the train rushing at you on the bridge. Then, there were the pink Sandwich long-stemmed wine glasses (which would be worth a fortune nowadays), though whatever they might be good for in this tee-totaling home might easily be wondered at. Also there was the stuffed owl with one eye slightly loose, which gave it a wild, fanatical stare which used to bother Glen at night when he was little. And, of course, there was the organ with its wild noises and the pumper which Grandma would often let him work. There were also some old coins which were brought out on occasion, as well as an album of photos and daguerrotypes which were exhibited on family gatherings.

But it was the celebration of Christmas tide which impressed Glen most about the old place. It was not like your ordinary Christmas which lasted but an evening and a day; this was a real country Christmas which began fully a week before and lasted twelve days afterwards until the proverbial twelfth night of January sixth. Glen and his mother would arrive on the Portland train from North Station about noon. They had transferred across Boston from the express section of the New York to Boston sleeper mail, which had pulled in to South Station that morning, as the sleepy but excited boy was bundled into a taxi for the short ride. Grampa Stone and the four-in-hand had driven down to town in the big rig which was large enough to seat six with baggage behind, and off they set for the farmhouse. Winter comes early in Maine, and the horses steamed as they pulled the heavy load through the drifting snow. When they got home they were welcomed and overwhelmed by a cascade, almost an avalanche, of aunts, who were both overjoyed to see them and astounded to find them safely through so many adventures of those dreadful, noisy trains.

It was several days yet to Christmas itself, but the whole house smelled like a bakery. The pantry was already packed with mince and pumpkin pies, apple pan dowdy, raspberry tarts, carrot cake, sponge cake, walnut cake, upside down cake, German fudge cake, and innumerable batches of cookies too variegated even to catalogue. Aunts Nettie and Nellie had been quarreling over which should have the honor of presenting the first cookies to Glen and his mother; and, of course, each had the ones she had baked to proffer. Glen diplomatically took some from each.

Then came the raising and trimming of the tree. Grampa had cut a large fir, just short enough to squeeze into the room and brought it in that afternoon from the back lot on the pung. First, the star was put on, then it was set up with supporting boards over a sheet immediately spread to catch the needles with cotton batting, some small pieces of which were saved out to be sprinkled on the branches. Then Bessie, Glen, and his mother sat down at the kitchen table and began to thread long strings of popcorn and cranberries. It took several hours before enough of them were done to satisfy the twins, and then they quarreled over which way the swirls of trimming should go: — Nettie said upward to the left, while Nellie wanted upward to the right. They compromised eventually on doing it both ways. Next came some small krinkly German trinkets, some red apples made into ornaments, and some paper stars. There was even an angel or two. But no candles, as Grampa felt they were very dangerous

68

on fir trees. The girls were allowed to put candles on the mantelpiece instead.

Christmastide also meant some relaxation in the strict rules about "no one allowed in the parlor". For after supper, led by Grampa and Grandmother, the whole family filed in. Grandma seated herself at the organ; Bessie handed out the hymnals, Grampa led the chorus, and they all sang Christmas carols. Glen was allowed to pump the organ while Grandma played it. It was a cozy scene. The formal room was warmly lit by kerosene hurricane lamps while the little family gathered round the organ; while outside the wind howled and the white snow drifted against the frosted window panes.

Each day seemed to have some added attraction. The venison was cut and consumed, the mince pie sampled, the presents wrapped amid great secrecy and whispering. Over it all a joyful fellowship prevailed, as if they were partakers in some great gigantic cosmic secret. On certain nights Nettie and Nellie were allowed to go out caroling with the church choir, and in due time the group would show up in the snow in front of the farm to sing "Holy Night", and "Jingle Bells."

At length, the evening of the great day itself arrived. The yule log had been brought in by the hired hands, sweating as they pushed its enormous breadth into the massive red fireplace. They were rewarded with a sip of egg nog — a teetotaling variety that Grandma supervised herself, though Glen observed when she was out in the kitchen, that Grampa slipped a dash of something from a hip pocket flask into his portion and those of the two hands. After toasts to Christmas, the hired men departed, and the family after prayers sat down to a roast suckling pig, a traditional repast on Christmas eve though Glen was disconcerted by the pig with a yellow apple in its mouth staring him in the eye.

After dinner and carols, stockings were hung by the chimney; candy, from fudge to pralines, was brought out; and Grampa read *"The Night before Christmas"* to the family with Glen sitting at his knee spellbound at this portrayal of Santa's imminent visit. Then it was time for Glen to be put to bed, with visions of sugar plums and other dainties dancing in his head as he went reluctantly to sleep.

Christmas Day dawned late in a blowing snowstorm, but the joy and happiness inside was complete. Grampa handed out the presents as they huddled around the tree in their robes. There were so many that by common consent there was a breakfast intermission while Glen was allowed to play on the floor with his toys.

Breakfast done, they returned to unwrap the last presents and then adjourned upstairs to dress for the day. Then it was to the kitchen to get ready for the Christmas feast, — a monstrous dinner which took several hours itself to prepare and lay on. First, there was the turkey, a twenty-pound giant, grown on the farm, prepared with oysters and chestnut dressing, and ably supported by a host of vegetables, including creamed corn, creamed onions, green peas, spinach, squash, turnips, rutabagas, cabbage, and lettuce, and of course, cranberry sauce. When these were on the table, the family assembled for the feast, with a preliminary blessing and toast in cider to the day. Then they fell to with a will and did dreadful damage to the turkey. At length, somewhat out of breath, and far more satiated, they restored conversation, and the girls cleared the table for the Christmas pudding. This was a rich concoction of butter, nuts, flour, eggs, raisins, and other more secret ingredients, steamed to a kind of suet all day long, and brought on in its stocking, still steaming from the pot.

A secret cream sauce (which in more liberal households would have been called a rum sauce) was poured over it, making the whole a delicious and tempting delicacy even for those already surfeited with food. Then out came the nuts, cheeses, cookies, tarts, pies, etc., enough to give anyone a stomachache just to look upon. Glen was severely cautioned by his mother not to have more than one of anything. Tired by the excitement and over-eating, most of the family quietly crept away to sleep in some corner, while Grampa snored peacefully on the divan. It had been a glorious Christmas.

★   ★   ★

In the summer of 1915, Glen was sent to Maine to be with his grandparents while his parents enjoyed a trip to Europe. They sailed on the Lusitania, and in a few days the dreadful news was flashed that they with many others had been lost at sea. While the news was a great blow to the family, it was much less severe for Glen than it otherwise would have been. He was with people he knew and liked and they all loved him. He felt much more at home on the farm than in the city, and so it was arranged that he should stay there. His grandfather always assumed that the disaster had been arranged by the Lord to punish Glen's parents for ever having met and married in the first place.

Glen spent the next few years with his grandparents, and at the local grade school. While he was the only child in the family, he did not lack for companionship. Outside the home he was social and affable and so acquired a number of local pals. After he completed grammar school, however, it became obvious that some new plans were necessary.

It had been decided that Glen should go to preparatory school, and Krampton had been selected. It was not far away, in the lake region of New Hampshire, — an old and established school for boys. Glen took the Boston train down to Dover, then changed to one for the Weirs, and then to Meredith, where he was picked up by the Krampton stage. He arrived one sunny fall afternoon at Krampton Village, home of the famous school, which had given so many graduates to state and national service. It was a charming little place, situated on an intervale on the banks of the Pemigewasset, with a little white country church in the crossroads, at one side of which were the Academy grounds, while on the other side were the general store, postoffice, and library which constituted, together with half a dozen white frame houses, the entire village.

A large hill stood behind the village; and as Glen came down over it, he spotted Brandall Hall, the principal dormitory and largest building. Handsomely built in red brick, it was nearly a century old, but still in excellent condition. Near by was the gymnasium and class building, and beyond that the administration and cafeteria building. These were all shaded by large elms, and set off with several green athletic fields extending behind them.

Glen was greeted by Broderick Brown, the famous and jovial headmaster, with a hearty laugh and a pleasant smiling face. Giving orders in a loud voice to several attendants, he soon had Glen snugly ensconsed in a dormer room in the big dormitory. Next Glen got his study and class card from J. C. Payne, the serious-minded registrar (known to the boys as "Racy-Jacy" because of his penchant for hurrying). He then went to the athletic building to get a locker, his sweat suit and to sign up for football. Here he met Pete, one of the villagers, and a general factotum, whose quaint dialect used to delight the athletes. Pete drove the athletic bus, known as the "mad hoosegow" because it had seats down each side, subway car style like a police van. Next Glen visited the bookstore to buy his books and supplies. This was presided over by "Clint" another local, who, as dog catcher, was the small town's only paid official, (He got his funds from the pound fees). Clint was also the town constable and marshal, a job he took far more seriously than the boys took him.

Glen's years at Krampton proved to be the happiest of his life. The school was small, and its academic standards not too rigorous. There was a lot of athletics and other extra-curricular activities, and most of all the New Hampshire outdoors which was tailor-made for skiing and hockey in Winter, and for hiking and tramping in the warmer seasons. There was a small-town friendliness in the village, which extended to the students, faculty and staff. It was like the enlarged family that Glen had become used to on his grandfather's farm. He got along well with his fellows, and while not a big-time athlete nor class leader, he was on most of the JV teams, and was considered a "good sport" by coaches and teammates alike. He rather liked the all-male atmosphere, since it simplified problems, and his male teachers were more tolerant of the natural rambunctiousness of boys than women teachers would have been. Glen struck up a friendship with a couple of spinsters, one of whom ran the town library, and who, in time, became like surrogate aunts to him. The years rolled by happily and uneventfully, and he actually had mixed emotions on the beautiful June morning that he graduated in ceremony on the lawn in front of the administration building.

From Krampton, Glen went to Dartmouth in a nearly New Hampshire town. His college days were routine; he joined the usual fraternity and got into the usual scrapes. The highlights, were, of course, the marvelous skiing, and the fabulous winter carnival, when eager coeds from Vassar and Smith came in armed with douche and diaphrams and were literally laid end to end in the upstairs fraternity bedrooms. It was a pleasant orgy, made more intense by booze which flowed copiously; but curiously, enough, it left Glen a little dissatisfied. It was, of course, wonderful to enjoy five or six different girls in order, but he found their frantic love-making a little disturbing, as if they were clutching after a closeness that such revels could not provide. Their sweet, silky bodies impassioned him, but they were, after all, much of a sameness. Somehow, he was being cheated, — and certainly the girls were, — in making love to someone in a drunken sexploitation whose name he did not even know. Glen's maturity began in that occasion when he realized that instantaneous bodily pleasure cannot fully compensate for the lack of knowing, sharing and loving.

Maturity got another assist when, in short order, Glen's grandparents died. The funerals brought to him a new kind of reality, — the transiency of human life; somehow he had expected them to live forever. The old home would never be the same without them; he was left with only his aunts to visit at the old place, but somehow both it and they seemed in some way diminished. He found solace in skiing.

At Dartmouth, one of his fraternity brothers was the son of a Standard Oil magnate, and Glen, together with his friend, spent summers working for the company. He was rewarded for this apprenticeship by being asked to join the firm upon graduation, which he did.

After a short training period the corporation promptly sent Glen to Maricaibo, Venezuela as an assistant to the company agent at the big operation there. The situation in Europe grew more and more ominous, and on his furloughs Glen went to Caracas for relaxation. The company was well-connected there, and Glen was invited to the Country Club where he attended the frequent dances. At several of these he met a beautiful young senorita, the daughter of a local shipping agent. It was mutual attraction at first sight, and after observing the proper Latin amenities, Glen was approved (partly because of his Standard Oil prospects), and admitted to serious suitorship. By this time he had asked her to marry him, and she had accepted, though their obvious ardor for each other was somewhat restrained by the strictures of Latin chaperonage.

Mercifully, they had a short engagement, as they both could hardly wait for the joys of the married state. After what seemed to each an age, but in reality was only a few months, the nuptial day arrived, and they were properly married in a lovely wedding Mass at the cathedral. To Glen, all of this was mumbo-jumbo, but he was willing to endure any rigamarole which resulted in his physical possession of this lovely girl's voluptuous body. Their honeymoon was a short trip to a beach hotel. Once ensconced in their suite, Glen knew that he would have to impassion his wife before he could take full possession of her. His collegiate experience came in handy.

Fresh from her bath, he laid her gently on the bed, knelt before her, and placing her legs over his shoulders, bent to her with his face, kissing the sacred spot lightly with his tongue. She did not know if she would live or die. With his hands on her nipples he manipulated her with his mouth in a steadily increasing crescendo of action. Her warmth became heat, and she began to moan and spasm. Roughly he grabbed her elbows making her feel completely helpless, all the time probing deeper and harder and beginning to nip. She could not stand any more, and began strange animal-like cries as her climax came, throwing back her head and up-thrusting her pelvis harder and harder to him, but still he would not let her loose. Finally with a shout of agonized joy she broke loose from him and rolled over, panting, moaning and sighing all at once.

They showered together, and she kissed him into another erection. He made a motion without any other communication, and she was down on her knees at the edge of the bed for him, chest bent low like a cat, her hips elevated, and her sweetness wet and ready. Seizing her from behind he thrust into her with a shout. Her eyes opened wide; her mouth parted, and she gave a little squeal at his immensity. She arched her back as he stood behind her, pumping ever faster, harder, and deeper. Never had man thrust his masculinity into more willing flesh than hers. Moans, sighs, tears and convulsions greeted his efforts. With gurgles of delight escaping her lips as he filled her completely, she begged him never to stop. Throwing her head back she rhythmically pushed herself against him until he seized her hands from behind and pinioned her down completely. She writhed with joy at this tight embrace, and her voice became a moan and then a scream as he continued ever faster. At length when neither could stand any more the coup-de-grace mercifully came, and they fell exhausted, entwined in sweet sleep.

Glen and Inez continued in this happy honeymoon estate for some time, but it began to be obvious that though they could tolerate bliss, they were hardly mature enough for problems. They were based back at Maricaibo, of course, to be near Glen's work; and the first hint of difficulty came with Inez' constant wish to visit her parents in Caracas, with whom she seemed unusually close — at least Glen thought so. She missed the glamour of the city itself, and would frequently go there alone over weekends when Glen was on duty in order to see her parents, and sometimes stay over for the next week also. Glen found this enforced bachelorhood after the joys of married life disconcerting.

Glen had expected that they would do everything together, and that the loneliness which overtakes most men in their twenties would be swallowed up in the warmth of this new relationship. It was certainly so whenever they made love, which was often, but, partly because of the language difference, there was little they could talk about, and the day-to-day intimacy in non-sexual matters, which develops as an adjunct to sexual closeness, did not make its appearance. There was nothing to do together except make love.

Even that had its problems. Being Catholic Inez took no precautions about pregnancy, — in fact she declared she would welcome the advent of a child, as did her parents; but despite frequent and ardent love-making she did not immediately conceive. Her parents started to ask questions on her visits there, and after returning from one of them she even accused Glen of being sterile.

Finally, mercifully, she became pregnant. But it was a difficult one; she had lots of morning sickness, and did not carry the child well. Naturally, she went home to be with her mother under these trying circumstances, and while there had a miscarriage. There were complications, and even when they were over, and she had returned to health and to Maricaibo, it was apparent that the marriage had been damaged.

"The doctors say that it would be dangerous for me to get pregnant again," she told him defiantly. It was obvious that she was afraid.

Since she would not use any birth control methods because of religious scruples, Glen found himself essentially without a wife, — at least one who would satisfy his sexual needs. Not only had he been cheated in not being given children, but now he was also cheated in not having a sex partner.

Furthermore, abstinence made Inez bitchy, and she would fly off the handle and blame Glen for anything that went wrong. She particularly never tired of telling him that he was responsible for her plight. Glen was reduced to considering that marriage was a trap. He even doubted that she had told him the truth about her medical advice. He considered taking a mistress, but even this prospect brought no thrill of anticipation, for he felt drained, empty, and passionless. Work was therapy for his wounds, and he engulfed himself in it, absenting himself from home more and more.

Then the War ended, but victory meant problems. Glen received notice that he was to be transferred to southern California. Inez did not want to leave her family in Caracas and refused to accompany him. Glen tried to resist the change, but could not do so, and eventually there was a separation, and finally a Mexican divorce.

Glen found Los Angeles very much to his liking. The weather was fine all year around. Business was booming. The girls were long-legged, pretty, sun-tanned, and accommodating. He set up a very contented life as a perennial bachelor, moving into an apartment eternally refreshed with breathless and fun-loving stewardesses.

This pleasant, but aimless life was occasionally punctuated by darker duties. His aunts, back East were dying; one had cancer, and the other high blood pressure, and both refused to have proper medical attention, depending instead upon faith cure. Glen was outraged that they should be so duped when medical care at least to prolong their lives was available. But his efforts were of no avail, and they both died. The whole affair left a certain miserableness, despair, and rancor in his heart.

He returned to the lighter and more frivolous life of grounding the stewardesses, but somehow it had lost some of its adolescent satisfactions. He had come upon a darker side of life for which there was no explanation. Ever since his parents' death he had avoided thoughts of dying. Now the experience had been pressed upon him directly. He was like an oyster with an irritating grain of sand.

Even in the sexual paradise of the apartment, Glen encountered a rude shock. One of the stewardesses "got religion" and refused to continue with the kind of desultory relations that Glen had become used to. As she was one of the most pleasant and satisfactory of his partners, her conversion annoyed Glen enormously. On the one hand he wanted to shake her; while on the other hand in order to placate her, he was forced to accompany her to one of the prayer meetings.

The leader of these meetings was a famous woman evangelist who was reputed to have remarkable powers, both to heal and to strike dumb. She appeared in dazzling white draperies amid a large entourage and chorus in an atmosphere much more reminiscent of a stage show than a prayer meeting. Needless to say, in Los Angles she attracted large crowds, most of whom were ecstatically in favor of her remarkable ministry.

Glen found himself both fascinated and repelled by this lady. He could not get her out of his mind. He also found that one never knows the value of water until the well runs dry; more specifically that it was the girl he could not have, instead of the multitude that he could bed for the

75

asking, which was the one he wanted. He feared he was falling in love with her. He even thought of asking her to marry him as a last resort. While his mind was thus disturbed with these contentions, fate played its trump card: the girl was killed in an air crash.

Glen was beside himself with emotion. Rage, sorrow and dispair were only a few of the feelings he felt. This latest disaster seemed just one more blow fate had in store for him, and all of a sudden he again had that panicky feeling that life was an empty charade. He wondered what the point of it all was. Life was like a gigantic catch-22 wherein destiny dealt him favors with one hand only to snatch them away with the other.

Eventually he found comfort in blaming the evangelical leader for the misery which had been gradually introduced into his life. He was predisposed to think that all such efforts were mere hokum and publicity designed to gather money and fame. He brooded about the injustice done his aunts, and, now, the tragedy which had befallen his sweetheart. Deciding to confront the evangelical leader in her own tabernacle, Glen went to the Sunday evening healing service. After many hymns and organ music the lady herself appeared in startling white against a beautiful rainbow-colored background, with a chorus in semi-circle praising the Lord. Glen could stand the hypocrisy no longer: rising from his seat he rushed forward down the aisle before any usher could prevent him.

Pointing his finger at the robed pastor, he shouted "You're nothing but an imp . . . . . ."

He got no farther. For the lady raised her hands, first with an accepting gesture, then shot one arm forward pointing at him and saying something unintelligible above the noise the commotion had caused.

He staggered back blinded by an internal flash of light. His head whirling, he crumpled against a chair. For an interior voice had spoken to him, saying "When you attack her, you persecute Me." In a half supine position, and blinded by the light, Glen's head slumped back, and he lost consciousness, cradled against the lap of one of the spectators. Ushers, used to this sort of experience, rushed him from the hall on a stretcher to a small anteroom where first aid was administered to those carried away by religious fervor.

It was some time before Glen recovered consciousness and found he was blind. This caused other incoherencies, so that a physician was called, who ordered him taken to a hospital for observation. Because Glen was still blind the next day, his case was diagnosed as hysterical blindness caused by shock; the nature of the shock was undefined.

If Glen's physical condition was parlous, his mental agitation may only be imagined. Confusion, anger, fear, doubt, dawning belief, stupefaction were only a few of the emotions raging in his mind which was unable to make any sense out of the whole matter. The fact of his blindness baffled him utterly; it was so undeserved.

There were two ways to go: one was to give up completely, since there was nothing to live for or to look forward to; the other was to restore some semblance of order to his mind by reviewing his life and seeking to find some meaning in it. The first insight he had was that his blindness was the first opportunity he had had to see his life in full perspective; it had forced him finally to take a look at himself. He began to realize that from the time of his parents' deaths onward, things had tended to happen to him without his having developed deep feelings about them.

It had been a long time since lasting emotions of caring, such as he had felt in his grandfather's home had surfaced in his experience. He welcomed them as old and forgotten friends. He realized that he had become callous in life, and that on those few occasions when he did have strong feelings, they were generally negative ones. Furthermore, it dawned on him that if he only had negative emotions (or worse, none at all) to the vicissitudes of his daily life; as a result he would naturally feel empty and depleted. One was the consequence of the other. He wondered why he had not seen all this before. He resolved to do better in the future.

As he was lying quietly in his bed one day in this mood, a great calmness seemed to descend upon him, and he seemed to hear the words "Peace, be still" form in his mind. Still rebellious, he queried the voice: "Why should I be still? I have nothing to live for." Again the voice formed in his mind. "If thou shall do MY work thou shall live and thou shall see." Somehow, this statement was made with such authority that Glen believed it. Almost immediately the tension was gone, and he lapsed into a prolonged and calm sleep.

When he waked the next morning the spirit was stirring within him. He decided to join the church, and asked for a visit from one of the temple attendants. When the man came to see him, he did not seem at all surprised by Glen's change of heart. Instead, he baptized Glen to the work of the church, and placing his hands on Glen's brow told him to rise and see in the strength of Jesus. Glen found that he was able to do so, — he could see, at first hazily, and gradually more and more clearly. Then something unexpected happened: Glen broke into an incoherent jumble of unintelligible speech, amid tears which seemed to wash his eyes clear again. "Now you have truly been baptized by the Holy Spirit" said the man, "For you have spoken in tongues."

True to his resolve, Glen took instruction eagerly and faithfully, and in a short time became an attendant and usher at the temple itself. The church and its work became the focus and center of his life and interest. He found in it complete satisfaction and contentment.

7 — GLEN

Bible readers will recognize this tale as paralleling the conversion and blinding of St. Paul on the road to Damascus. A late famous evangelist in Los Angeles was reputed to have this "zapping" power on suitable occasions.

CHAPTER 8
Schroeder

Disgustedly, Schroeder threw the offending book across the quiet library, just missing the fireplace. He was thoroughly annoyed with this continued nibbling at the basis of classical physics. Zukav's *The Dancing Wu Li Masters* was only the latest of a series of books on science by Capra, Sagan, and others, (or as Schroeder more accurately put it on pseudo-science) which revolted his orthodox nature. One could ascribe the maunderings of Stanford's Research Institute, as seen in the divagations of Puthoff and Targ to the balmy effect the California climate must have on the minds of those temerious enough to live there, but enough was enough. He had seen one science after another pervaded by half-baked ideas, — psychic archeology, continental drift in geology, social biology, the *Territorial Imperative,* Jayne's *The Origin of Consciousness in the Breakdown of the Bicameral Mind,*[1] but the assault now was on physics herself.

Schroeder's background naturally fitted him for such an opinion. He was the son of a well-known *Ausserordentlicher nich beamteter* Professor (Associate professor without civil service rank) in the classics department of a large German University (which was as far as a Jewish scholar could be expected to go). They had not been close, for as the only son, Schroeder had always felt threatened by the pressure to live up to (or perhaps maybe somehow surpass) his father's brilliance and expertise. Having conjugated his way through a classical German gymnasium, Schroeder chose to go to university in America, and to reduce the conflict of family pressure; he also chose as opposite a field as possible, namely theoretical physics. Concerned about the future of his son in the Nazi regime, the father had allowed him to go, but had himself been caught when the war broke out, and nothing more had been heard from him. All that Schroeder had was the completed manuscript of his father's last work, — a trilogy on the development of the psyche, somewhat in manner of Rank and Jung. The MS brought back sad and bad memories, and Schroeder filed it away.

Fortunately he had learned English at the gymnasium, and this coupled with his natural bent for science took him swimmingly through a famous Eastern University, with a *summa* in physics at 19, followed by an early doctorate at MIT, and eventually the chief physicist in charge of quality control in a large and prestigious U.S. Corporation. At 60, comfortably married, and at the top of his profession, he was (or should be) in the catbird seat. Mendelev was in his heaven and all was right with the world. Or should have been, but Schroeder was vaguely dissatisfied, and he took his dissatisfaction out on ideas with which he did not agree, chief of which was a non-positivistic look at science in general and physics and chemistry in particular.

One would think that Socrates had been dead long enough so that some of his outmoded and simplistic ideas (and worse ill-fitting metaphors) could finally be laid to rest. But no, the Allegory of the Cave (for example) persisted, and had even been given modern respectability by the likes of professor Bohm[2] of London with his implicate/explicate theory. One had laughed for years at the quaint pretentions of Christian Science, and the practitioner who found herself in hell but "wasn't really there". But there was a certain disquieting tendency afoot to controvert the reality of the senses (and hence of classical physics) with a modernized Berkeleyian idealism. While this heresy was mainly the product of California acid-heads, it had somehow permeated into somewhat more respectable channels.

To be fair one must admit that science had cooperated in some degree in this onslaught on its most sacred shibboleths. The trouble had really started with Planck and Einstein who had so uprooted classical physics that the complementarity principle had to be invoked. And if two mutually contradictory statements are possible at the same time in physics, why not elsewhere? Clearly this was the embarrassment of the matter. And the vagaries of the quark theory which allowed for the spontaneous creation and annihilation of a virtual particle, (whatever *that* might be), did not help matters in the slightest. Things had been so clear and ordered up to 1900. God knows where the 20th Century would end up.

But an even darker fear/suspicion possessed Schroeder. Suppose it should be discovered that the quantum principle applied not only to the Heisenberg constant, but indeed to all of existence. Suppose there were quanta of not merely of energy and light, but of all objects which had magnitude, not merely of atoms, but of people, of love, and rage, and even consciousness, — in short of everything. How would we then need to alter our perception of nature? Support order and disorder were somehow quantasized? The disorder instead of becoming infinitesimally diluted in a system of nearly total order would split into two subsystems, one with all the remaining disorder, and the other with no disorder in it at all but in total order. What would the properties of such a divided system be? He thought worriedly of the two fluid model as illustrated by liquid helium below the Kelvin point, with the superfluidity and superconductivity displayed by one of the fluids. Were those miraculous characteristics merely the result of ordinary laws in extraordinary situations? Was this simple example merely an earnest of the spectactular discoveries ahead? It was all very perturbing and confusing. He felt as if once solid ground was liquefying under him.

Somehow this all reminded Schroeder of the rough draft and notes his father had left behind, — a book in a sense about a higher order of reality than science was able to discern, — something which Spinoza might have touched upon. The whole idea of a reality not tangible to the senses was distasteful, so Schroeder began to reminisce about his interactions with his father, — those few occasions, when as a small boy, he was seated on his father's knee, and read to from Goethe's and Heine's poetry, some Shakespeare, and the tale he loved best *Aladdin and the Wonderful Lamp*. The magic cave, presided over by the fierce but compliant genie seemed very real to him in those days. He also recalled the Sunday night sings with his mother at the piano. His father had a deep bass voice, and Schroeder loved to sing along in his treble. He found himself humming the air from one of the songs, which just seemed to arise by itself in his mind. As he sank deeper into his reverie he felt again the awe of his father's brilliance and intensity, — a sensation that so often overwhelmed him whenever he stood within his father's presence, both when he was a child, and now as an adult some 50 years later, just remembering those bygone days. Another refrain kept occuring to him, and he hummed that one also.

As he sat dreamily considering these matters, all of a sudden, he became aware that the library room was illuminated with light as if one were to light up a Christmas tree in a darkened chamber. He had had on only a small reading lamp, so the change was very noticeable. It was not the light of day; it was more warm and colorful, and Schroeder could not see where it came from, for it seemed to cast no shadow. As he examined the phenomenon more closely, now his interest had been engaged and his mind recalled from its revery, to his utter amazement, he found that the light issued from his own body![3] But what a thing this was, this sudden illumination, impossible, yet a fact! It was on the one hand so intangible, and yet its significance at once struck in his mind like a thunderclap. It had no relation to ordinary light, but instead it was as if (and Schroeder blanched to think the expression) he had suddenly been illuminated by the presence of God.[3] Certainly he was enveloped in a palpable living fire, which however, gave only the gentlest heat, but a curious rushing sound, as of the wind blowing.[4] Then with that unfolding glory, there came a suffusion, as of a delicate cloud or haze, which searching his entire body was more invasive than light, more penetrating than heat, and more inreaching then electricity.[4] It was as if he had been plunged into a plasma, — a bath of fluid more subtle and permeating than ether. Furthermore his hair was raised, and his fingers and toes pricked. Looking at his hands, he observed faint rays of fire which seemed to emanate from the finger tips. It seemed to him also that he could detect some electrical smell, perhaps that of ozone.

Observing this, he immediately concluded that whatever was happening to him, was at least partly electrical in nature, not unlike the Crookes discharge from the partial vacuum of a cathode ray tube, and that he was in no immediate danger of electrocution, though what might cause such an anomaly of nature was quite beyond him. Determined nevertheless to keep his composure, and observe the phenomena carefully as all good scientists should, he looked again at his hands, and found them to be almost translucent, as if the illumination came from below the skin, and rendered the cuticle more or less transparent. Accompanying the radiance was a soft, gentle heat, which was not in the least unpleasant physically, but whose cause and source, as of the light, perplexed Schroeder's scientific mind greatly. Could the principle of non-locality apply to such mysterious energy? Why did it not cast a shadow? Was he somehow dreaming the whole thing?

If this is not hallucination, Schroeder thought, then he must find some way to verify, record or measure this effect. He must secure a witness, or otherwise validate the authenticity of the event. There was, however, no one else in the house. "Perhaps if I go and telephone a friend" he said to himself, "I can get oriented." Meanwhile the interior light continued, so that in the darkness, he seemed to illuminate the room as much as the wattage from a small Christmas tree would light up such a place. Reaching for the phone to call up a friend, he became conscious, all at once, (he did not know how), that there was a presence in the room. He saw nothing, he heard nothing, but something deep within him knew its coming.

This presence filled the room with a kind of overwhelming grace, so that it was not possible to be afraid, concerned, or even curious any more. But in a strange way it was both inside him and outside him at the same time; ("more non-locality" he thought to himself), and yet he felt that he was more himself than ever before. He became filled with an intense happiness, and almost unbelievable joy, such as he had never known before or since. It was like discovering that all one's long lost relatives, family and friends are once again safe in one's midst. And over all was a deep sense of peace, security and certainty.

But the electrical pyrotechnics were mere epiphenomena to the transformation produced in Schroeder's mind. There was no argument about the reality of this experience; it had a validity of its own which passed that of even sight itself. It was not merely real in the sense that one knows waking reality from a dream. It was supremely real, as if waking reality were the dream from which he had awakened. Socrates was right after all; he had been looking at the shadows; now he was for the first time seeing the sunlight in all its blinding beauty. As he watched his whole previous conceptualization of the universe dissolve away, he realized in a flash that it was only necessary to adjoin to it a larger vivency of an ulterior reality of which it was merely a single sub-system. The cave-shadows are a kind of reality until one had glimpsed the sunlight; moreover, the sunlight orients one to the limits of the cave; it does not negate its existence.

[5]Directly upon this recognition, came a sense of exultation, joy and uplift, immediately followed by an emotional illumination quite impossible to describe.[5][6] In that second, his doubts about the goodness of the universe, the existence of a Supreme Power, and the immortality of life all were resolved by some kind of inner assurance, so powerful and overwhelming that it literally changed his life and way of thinking. He knew that the cosmos is a living presence, that the soul of man is immortal, that the universe is so ordered, that all things work together for good, and that the foundation of this is love. The illumination resolved doubts and issues which had troubled him for years. It was an instantaneous initiation into a new and higher order of ideas and wisdom.[6]

He, who had been an agnostic and a free thinker, inclined to the hard positivism of material science, in that instant became converted to a wider and more spiritual view of life. And the effect was as total as it was instantaneous. It was as if a gigantic veil had been drawn aside, and he had been privileged to see into the depth of all things. it was earth-shaking and awe-inspiring. He felt blessed, happy, joyous, redeemed, safe, fortunate and at peace with the world. No longer did he need any exterior validation of the matter; the proof was internal: he knew its certainty in his soul.

Then something suddenly changed as if a curtain had been drawn aside, or a slide had been removed from the projector in a slide show. All at once in place of the material objects in the surround there were little points of light, like small shining diamonds. An accompanying illumination told him at the same moment that he was seeing what Teilhard de Chardin had called "the within," instead of the "without" of things. For he somehow understood then, that in all things in the universe, in atoms no less than man, there is a spark of consciousness, however low, a spark of Divine Fire, which is not manifested in our realm of time and space, but is in place in the higher vivency of potentiality, from which our material realm manifests itself. He remembered that indeed the poet Rilke had called it the *Weltinnenraum,* the inner space of the world. Schroeder then realized he had been privileged to have the physical hologram dissolve before him, so that he could examine in this rare moment its infrastructure. He thought of Bohm's distinction between the inner implicate mode, and the outer explicate mode, and realized that he had been privileged to view a transition. Simultaneously, he understood why men prized jewels, since they and they alone conveyed to the physical world the fire, shine, and glow of this inner and usually hidden arcana.

This extreme euphoria, similar to, but certainly much greater than that after sexual congress, stayed with him for some time, so that he was not conscious of the passage of time, but remained in a dreamy rapturous state, in great gratitude for the benison which had been afforded him. At length he came to himself with a start and noticed that he was sitting as before with only a reading light in the room. The Divine Fire had left him but he was a changed man as a result.

The vision left his mind unusually clear, and matters which he had been confused about for a long time, became suddenly perfectly simple. Reality, he now realized is properly everywhere. When we attempt to "locate" it in time and space; we pay a penalty; this penalty is the "location" charge of gravitation. It is acquired in any interaction which confers rest mass, and is a consequence of breaking vacuum symmetry with respect to energy distribution. In a flash of intuition, Schroeder saw that this breakthrough of thinking allows gravitation to be treated like the other three primal forces of physics. In a creative revery he went to this typewriter and wrote out the following statement.

[7]Recent efforts toward unification of the four natural forces have met with success in the electroweak theory (Goldhaber et all 1980, Salam, 1980, Weinberg). The strong force may soon be included in this scheme but gravity remains outside the common format. This paper addresses the problem of the relationship of gravitation to the other forces and suggests a means for a conceptual unification.

All forces, except gravitation, have defined, conserved charges (flavor, electric charge and color) and all, except gravitation, are presumed to acquire these charges through a process of vacuum interaction known as spontaneous symmetry-breaking (SSB). I will propose a gravitational charge and symmetry-breaking mechanism which will allow us to model gravity as we do the other forces. With these additions, Einstein's theory is accepted throughout.

I suggest the name 'location' for the gravitational charge. The location charge is a specification of some xyzt, a particular combination of vacuum dimensional scalors. Vacuum dimensional scalors are here placed in direct analogy with the Higgs vacuum scalors of flavor charge in the weak force SSB mechanism. The dimensions are also energetic scalors of the charged vacuum, awaiting specification. Yang-Mills photons which acquire rest mass through the weak force SSB mechanism will also acquire location charge through an analogous process.

The location charge arises whenever particles acquire rest mass, through whatever process. Since a particle with rest mass must be located at some specific xyzt, the location charge is an inevitable companion of that condition. Regardless of what other vacuum symmetries are broken during the acquisition of rest mass, whether that of color, flavor or electric charge, a more universal vacuum symmetry is also broken, that of the distibution of energy within the vacuum. The symmetrical condition of vacuum energy distribution is uniformity everywhere; but particles with rest mass are concentrations of energy at a specific location — hence they break the vacuum symmetry with respect to the uniform distribution of energy, resulting in the acquisition of location charge. The magnitude of this charge is proportional to the total energy density of rest mass, that is, to the magnitude of symmetry-breaking.

A physical characteristic distinguishing particles with location charge is their lack of intrinsic motion, the condition we imply by 'rest' mass. Particles without rest mass, such as the photon, move intrinsically at velocity C. Such particles have no location charge. The evidence for this is just that relativistic requirement that clocks stop and meter sticks shrink to nothing at velocity C. In other words, the xyzt's vanish at C and the photon has no location — it is literally everywhere at once, in its own reference frame. The photon represents the symmetric condition of energy distribution in the vacuum; the velocity C is just that condition which satisfies vacuum symmetry with respect to energy distribution. (A photon captured by the electron shell of an atom would acquire location upon capture).

The graviton is the field vector of the location charge, just as the photon is the field vector of the electric charge. Unlike the photon, however, which couples to other electric charges, the graviton couples directly to the vacuum dimensional scalors rather than to other masses. The effect is the production of a local energy metric, or guage. The wholly energetic character of this metric is formalized by the inclusion of C in each dimensional term of the Lorentz-Einstein transformations of coordinate systems, whether x,y,z, or t. The local energy metric which results determines that the rate at which a clock ticks will be related to its size, when the same clock is compared in different gravitational fields. Gravity is not a particle x particle force; it is a particle x vacuum force, first represented as such by Einstein. The gravitational equations of General Relativity represent the force as a distortion of the spacetime metric, rather than an interaction between masses. It is for this reason that gravity bends light even thought the photon has no location charge, and that gravitational shielding is impossible.

The vacuum dimensional scalors are not fictitious, they are encountered in our daily lives, experienced as the 'g' forces of turns (x,y,z) and accelerations (t). The energetic content of x,y,z as well as t is here a commonplace. These inertial forces, formalized by Newton in his laws of Motion, constrain us to move in straight lines at constant velocities. These rules of motion do not reside in ourselves, they are externally imposed upon us by the dimensional scalors of the vacuum. Spacetime is a 4-dimensional subset of the N-dimensional vacuum metric; spacetime and the vacuum metric are the same structure to the limit of 4 dimensions, the limit of our interaction. This identity was formalized by Einstein in his Principle of Equivalence of gravitational and inertial mass; the graviton couples to the same metric through which we move. The relationship between the 4 dimensions is given by Einstein's spacetime Interval: $dS^2 = dX^2 + dY^2 + dZ^2 - C^2dT^2$. The conserved quantity S^2, the Interval, indicates that the 4 dimensions form an integrated whole; we cannot think of the 4th term T as simply added to three pre-existing spatial terms, the four together are an inseparable unit.

The energy metric produced by the gravitational couple has local symmetry; the Equivalence Principle holds for the Moon as well as the Earth, only the local gauge is different. A major effect of this couple is the fabrication of an energy map of the location of all particles with rest mass in the Universe. The energy map consists of the least-energy pathways of curved spacetime (actually straight lines), which point unambiguously toward the center of mass of bound particles. Visualized as a mapping problem, we can formulate a least-energy argument for attractive rather then repulsive gravity: it takes less energy to map many particles at a single point. All particles of the Earth's mass are mapped at one point, the center of mass. Repulsive gravity would produce a very complicated map. A symmetry argument may also be advanced for attractive gravity: in the primordial Universe, when (presumably) matter and antimatter were equally abundant, attractive gravity would serve to bring these two forms together, reducing bound states to their more symmetrical condition, photons. The location charge implies that there is no gravitational difference between particle and antiparticle: since the location of either is given in terms of ± xyzt, the squared terms of the spacetime Internal will not distinguish location from antilocation.

The gravitational charge is here seen to work like any other charge: particles have location, antiparticles have antilocation, matter-antimatter annihilations cancel charges, producing neutral photons.

Our most immediate experience of the gravitational couple to the vacuum metric is our sensation of 'weight' on the Earth's surface. The warped metric produced a preferred energy pathway toward the center of the Earth. The energy metric urges us in its compelling terms to follow this path. Since we cannot fall through the Earth's solid surface, we experience the 'g' forces of the accelerated (warped) metric. Einstein's Principle of Equivalence is also a statement of the relativity of warped metrics: it makes no difference whether the metric is accelerated through us, or we accelerate through it; energetically, the result is the same since the warp is the same.

It is useful to note the striking similarity of the four forces' charge and conservation systems. The spacetime xyzt's are confined partial charges which have no separate existence or conservation; only the whole charge unit, the Interval, is conserved in every frame of reference. Similarly in the other forces, flavor, electric charge and color are not separately conserved within the confined system of quark partial charges; only the whole units of charge, the neutrinos (flavor), charged leptons (flavor and electric charge) and the baryons (flavor, electric charge and color) are wholly conserved free particles.

A quark is a collection of 3 partial charges, flavor, electric charge, and color. A single quark cannot be free since no fractionally charged conservation quanta exist; there are no neutrinos for the individual quark flavors, no fractionally charged leptons, no free single colors. Conservation applies instead to the whole quark system, known as baryon number. However, flavor changes within the quark system do occur in fundamental whole charge units of electrical and flavor charge, conserved as leptons. In beta decay, a D quark changes to a U quark, a change of one lepton charge unit for both flavor and electric charge. The flavor charge splits into flavor (Ve), carried by the electron, and antiflavor (V̄e), which escapes as a free particle, having no uncancelled charges. The electron remains bound to the nucleus, however, due to its uncancelled electric charge. it would appear that the flavor charge has annihilated itself, but this is not so; the two halves exist in different states and cannot in fact annihilate due to the electric charge of the electron. For bookkeeping, flavor is said to be conserved by the lepton number of the electron. Like the baryon, the electron is a 'hung' particle because of its multiple charges. The electron cannot cancel its electric charge in the nucleus because it would have to cancel its flavor charge also; that cancellation is impossible due to the escaped neutrino. On the other hand, the electron cannot completely escape the nucleus due to its electrical charge.

No analog of the lepton system is known for color, although a high-energy process may exist (Glashow 1980). I suggest, however, that an analogous system does exist for location. In this case the photon plays the role of the neutrino, doing for the location charge what the neutrino does for the flavor charge. When mass annihilates and converts to photons, the xyzt's of the location charge vanish; but just as the neutrino carries a quantum whole unit of a vanished quark flavor charge, so the photon carries a unit of the vanished location charge. When the neutrino encounters a suitable quark system, it can recreate the flavor charge unit which it carries. Likewise the photon, when captured by the electron shell of an atom, acquires its location charge again, in consequence of its bound condition. The xyzt's reappear, the atom gains energy and rest mass, and the volume of spacetime enclosed by the electron shell increases. This increment of spacetime and the energy associated with it is the quantum whole unit of location. The photon is the lepton of location, conserved as the Interval.

I have shown, in conceptual form, how gravitation may be included in current models of the forces. The postulated location charge is identified as the causative agent of the force, arising as a consequence of a broken vacuum symmetry, that of the uniform distribution of energy. The mechanism by which the charge is acquired is analogous to that of the acquisition of flavor in the weak force SSB mechanism: dimensional scalors latent in the vacuum are specified as the location charge in any process which confers rest mass. Location appears to be compatible with Einstein's formulation of General Relativity, and the system of charges and conservation laws for gravitation is seen to be similar to that for other forces.[7]

★   ★   ★

This statement, when published, launched Schroeder into a new phase in his career. It was hailed as a breakthrough by some, and denounced by other; all agreed that it was something new, and considerably different from his earlier writing. It would take us too far afield to trace the scientific ramifications of this document and the ensuing controversy. It is enough to say, that Schroeder himself was aware that something new and in a certain sense alien had been introduced into his thinking: it was almost as if his father had used Schroeder's mind to document some of his more outré theories.

The cognitive bridge which reminded Schroeder of his father's work was that they both had tried to unify the separate "realities" of the universe, — his father in psychological terms, and he in physical. He was impelled to retrieve his father's manuscript, but this time to read it with renewed understanding from a different and larger point of view. To his amazement he saw exactly how the implications of his paper bore on his father's work, and decided then and there that he would edit and publish the latter in some final form. He also gained a deep sense of relatedness, and awareness of profound love for his father. This realization brought a lasting sense of peace, which carried with it no regret, but rather a welcomed release through the feeling of identity or affinity. His own self-esteem was heightened in the process, and he began to feel a sense of wholeness.

The results of all this was that Schroeder now saw his own work in a new light, to be done not for the recognition which might derive from it, or the benefits he might experience, but more impersonally for the overall development of mankind's understanding of the universe and his part in that unfolding. He would finish the job which his father had started of unifying the separate realities of nature and man, and bringing them into harmony and order.

8 — SCHROEDER

[1]See references.

[2]For Bohm see Zukav (1979:323-29), and index there.

[3]Gowan (1975:359 quoting Th. Merton *The Ascent of Truth* Harcourt Brace, (1965:278-9).

[4]Bucke (1901) also 1923:330 quoting M.C.L.

[5]Bucke's own illumination (Bucke 1901:v) as quoted by Gowan (1975:362). Schroeder's experience parallels that of Pascal (see Bucke 1901:274) who was also surrounded by fire. Cf Moses' experience with the burning bush on Mt. Sinai, (*Exodus* 3:2-5).

[6]More by Bucke (1901:10) speaking in third person of his own illumination.

[7]From an unpublished paper by son, J.A. Gowan, titled "Location: the charge of Gravitation," reprinted by permission.

CHAPTER 9
Winston

Winston was a young man given to visions; it had not always been so. He had started as merely a bright youth with a large vocabulary, a yen for reading, and a flair for poetry. In grammar school he was rather a loner and a dreamer, as he was skipped several grades. But with adolescence he came into his own as a tall, well-favored youth with high ideals who seemed particularly attractive to girls. He was not especially athletic, though a very good student, but he had a certain off-hand and original way of doing things and saying things which bore the charm and stamp of creativity. He was also possessed of a mature and judicial frame of mind which constantly weighed the alternatives in any sort of ethical dilemma, and even seemed to enjoy doing so. This was a rare talent in post World War II youth.

One of the first of these which occurred was a conflict over high ideals versus overt sexual behavior. Even before the flood tides of his own maturing masculinity impassioned his thinking, earlier maturing girls had begun to notice his broad shoulders and handsome face, and he began to be concerned with such questions as whether you should kiss a girl merely to make her happy if you didn't love her, or how honest it was to tell her you loved her anyway.

Adolescence also brought Winston face to face with the other great abstract nouns — life, truth and immortality. Not satisfied with the sectarian religion of his parents or playmates, he began to read widely in comparative religions, including the Eastern ones. Upon reading such material, he began to become accustomed to passing into a state of deep revery wherein the various points pro and con on matters of ethics and morals would be thrashed out in his mind. If God was good why did He permit evil in the world? Is there justice in one man's being brighter or richer or healthier than another? Was Jesus the true saviour of the world or just another prophet? Is divorce morally permissible; and, if so, under what conditions? Are war and killing another human being ever jutified?

Under what conditions is sex between man and woman permitted morally? Is homosexuality an evil? Would we be better off not eating meat? These were a few of the large questions which occuped his mind. It would not be correct to say that they tormented him but one could certainly say that he was somewhat obsessed by them. He was the more concerned, as none of his fellows seemed to understand his concern.

About this time, he began to have overt sexual experiences with girls, going beyond the kissing stage.

On one occasion his sister had invited one of her girl friends to stay at the house. Grace was a somewhat stocky young woman with a full figure, which in a few years would become fat, but which in her adolesc ence was voluptuous. One night after a dance, he was going by the bathroom when she motioned for him to come inside. She was dressed only in her bra and panties, and he was quite embarrassed to be with her under such circumstances.

"Wouldn't you like to see them?" she asked, pulling off her bra and revealing two beautiful round white breasts, very full.

He was fascinated; and sitting on the edge of the tub, he drew her to him and gently fondled them in combined bliss and shock.

"Wouldn't you like to kiss them?" she asked, holding one of them out to him cupped in her hand so as to offer the nipple. Overjoyed, he willingly took it in his mouth and began to suck hard. She had a large red nipple surrounded with a sizeable aureole which looked almost inflamed. He continued to nurse her, putting his hand on her other breast. Giving a sigh, she sank down on his knee.

"No, no, feel me, feel me," she whispered, placing his hand on her upper leg. He was too embarrassed to put it inside her panties, but he began instinctively to rub her pubis. She was visibly affected, gave a shiver and a sigh, and put his hand away. Kissing him on the lips, she motioned for him to leave her. He was too confused and embarrassed to do anything else.

As a result of this incident, Winston developed a crush on Grace, and she was top girl for two whole weeks. It was characteristic of him to burst into poetry:

"There's a song in my soul which no trouble can still;
There's a new bit of Spring in my heart.
There's a lift in my stride as I work with a will,
Which nothing but love can impart.

There's a brightness, a lightness, a joy in my face;
There's a swing and a spring in my voice.
There's a new joi de vivre which can only take place

When there's something in which to rejoice.

What is it this something, which quickens me through?
And fills me with hopes from above?
Why darling, you know it's the sweet thought of you,
Your self, and your heart and your love.

There's a song in my soul which will sing through the years,
No matter where fate shall incline;
It's a song about us, beyond laughter or tears,
A song which your soul taught to mine.

This was Winston's entrance into the happy-sad, never-never land of promiscuous heterosexuality, in which he found himself in love often with several girls at a time, or could not make up his mind which one to date next. Each evanescent love-affair had to be celebrated with a poem, or several, if Winston could get them written before the crush cooled off, or the girl deserted him for a football player. Here are three sonnets written to the red-headed Esther who in ten days time jilted him.
The first:

Before you came I lived a cynic's life
With scoffs and platitudes my daily fare
And oft when doubt had deepened to dispair
From sheer inertia kept the weary strife.
What profited it all? — this bootless fight
To keep myself forever clean and true?
When all that met my oft-discouraged view
Was ever-darker clouds and deeper night.
But when you came to me like welcome dawn
Who with her lantern lights the dawning day
Your brilliance bathed in bliss a mind forlorn.
I found myself within its genial ray
My answer came. My vision then reborn
Soared larklike to its morning ecstasy.

The second, a few days later:

Dear when in song I sing you hymns of praise
I mean not you but she you represent.
The poet celebrates her winsome ways:
The man finds you his source of sentiment.
She is my Goddess. All that I hold high

93

Shall in her light shine forth before all man.
My secret thoughts in her find their reply.
With her I find my faith and hope again.
You are the priestess who now holds the shrine
At which I worship; may you always keep
Its altars holy, this respect of mine
For her still high, and love for you still deep.
To say in short what I have said above.
Her I adore: you are the one I love.

And finally at the end of the infatuation:

When I have held you in our last embrace
And on the morrow can but call you friend
When time has brought his ill-considered end
Which e'en all memories soon seeks to erase,
When love is dying on a bed of pain
With ashes, rose leaves ashes, all around
Dropped from my bleeding heart upon the ground
And all is over, ne'er to return again,
Then shall I mourn your passing with that pride
An army pays its fallen potentate
Musing on former victories by his side
As solemnly his bier they venerate,
Proud of his life, and of the death he died,
Do him all honour as he lies in state.

Winston realized that he needed some definite sexual mores to follow. He would not have sexual intercourse with a girl without taking his own precautions. Mutual gratification was allowable, however; and petting to orgasm was permitted without any explicit love declaration. Furthermore, he did not wish to be the one to take a girl's virginity, and he was seriously concerned about the responsibility of impregnating a girl. He recognized correctly that it was as much the man's responsibility to prevent this, as it was the girl's so it seemed better on the whole, not to put the pressure of anxiety and indecision on someone he cared for.

Most adolescent girls were very satisfied with mutual masturbation and petting to climax. He learned quickly how to finger them gently below, while he kissed their lips or nipples. Generally they liked considerable interior exploration, but occasionally the delicate membrane of virginity would bar the slender aperture, and he would content himself and them with a gentle massage of the clitoris. He learned that patience and tenderness, and a good deal of generalized stroking was very satisfying to most girls, and also that there were wide differences in the strength of the libido, the number of orgasms desired, and the placidity or violence of the spasm itself. Winston also found himself almost clinicially interested in the minutiae of the menstrual cycle, keeping track of the girls, sometimes much to their embarrassment.

Winston experienced for the first time in his life, the "observer" phenomenon. It was as if there were two parts of his consciousness, — the hotly-impassioned youth immersed in the enjoyment of lovemaking and celebrating that joy in poetry, and the abstract clinician, disinterestedly observing all that goes on, making mental notes, and motivated only, like any professional, to improve his skill and knowledge so as to maximize the comfort and welfare of his client.

In the Spring when a young man's fancy turns to thoughts of love, and the poet and lover was in the ascendant in Winston, he took a cuddly coed named Taffy for a nature walk, during which there was considerable kissing and petting. The only permanent result was the following.

Spring Song

Our love was born in hills of blue
When Spring ruled mistress over all
Then we with Nature saw her too
And heard together her soft call.

Then arm in arm we walked entranced
Thru ferny forests newly green
While romping rivulets downward danced
And azure skies looked down serene.

And hand in hand we looked with awe
At all of Nature made anew
And in its manifestoes saw
Spring's call to us to follow too.

Our love was born in hills of blue
When spring ruled mistress over all
Then we with nature saw her too
And heard together her soft call.

It would be a great mistake to conclude that Winston's sole interest was in sex. He was fascinated by the mystery in many commonplace things: the homing instinct in pigeons, the language of ants and bees, why a constant wind blowing over an otherwise smooth sea will produce waves of a particular height and fetch, why water expands when it freezes, the diffraction of light rays, the mysteries of the bionomial expansion, the different kinds of crystals, the operation of the human brain, the part played by interferon, quasars and pulsars, the correspondences between Roman history and our own, the derivation of words, and the putative existence of angels or other beings above man in some Divine scale.

But it was the girls themselves who could not seem to let Winston alone. One night at a summer camp where he was a counselor, three girls from the adjoining camp invited him over to their tent. Much to his surprise, they insisted on holding a nude beauty contest with Winston the judge. There was much giggling, posing, and vying for his favor. At length after a number of sights well calculated to excite any young man, he declared he could not choose between them. It was then decided that he should be blindfolded and feel each girl in turn, not knowing who was who, until he had picked a winner. Not surprisingly, this led to a good deal of foreplay and eventually to petting to climax.

On another occasion, Winston took a girl out for a petting session on the lake. They started with a nude swim, and increased their ardor by clinging to each other in the water. As he took her onto the beach and started to explore her manually, she indicated that she wanted him to kiss her there instead. Surprised, he obeyed, which seemed quickly to drive her to an explosive orgasm, and even more surprisingly excited him tremendously so that he had a strong erection. She took hold of him and, bending down, began to suck him vigorously, and obviously with relish. He was astonished that she wanted him like this, the more so since the act disclosed to him that the impulse was instinctive rather than an artifice of perverted learning. Under her soft lips he quickly came to climax and sleepy enfolded contentment, though in general he found the act too passive fo his masculine nature.

For Winston, heterosexuality was not a forbidden sweet, but an intrinsic celebration of love and life. It evoked tenderness and concern in him, rather than the "scoring" exploitation of some of his fellows. It helped him know and see the values in a girl, and it aided him in prizing her for her outstanding qualities, and in understanding her feelings of inferiority and weakness (which he was surprised to find the entire sex had). He was enabled often to sense nascent strengths which would bloom at maturity and to help girls develop them. He was surprised at the lack of control which many felt as a result of the biological responsitilities which had been visited upon them, but which they were loathe to assume. It gave him increased empathy with the way girls thought and tried to solve problems — ways which were so often different from his own; and he was further amazed that so many of them did not consciously try to solve problems at all, but simply drifted.

So sexual attraction and love for Winston became a service of learning about feelings and caring about needs. He counted his successes not by the number of orgasms he was able to induce in a girl, but by the increased control and stability she attained through his constant attention and compliments. He discovered that he could never overdo praise for the weak and developing egos, and he became constant and generous in telling the girl that he loved her. This valuing seemed to make her bloom. Her face would light up with prettiness, and she would blossom all over like the rose.

At the same time as his sexual explorations Winston carried on an intensive investigation of things spiritual, reading widely and cogitating deeply. He saw no discrepancy between the love of God and the love of God's creatures: girls. His mysticism was very much that of the medieval minstrels — a mysticism of love, which was one whether expressed in its highest or lowest forms. He saw in love of girls a tenderness and compassion, a caring for their needs, weaknesses and infirmities, a concern for their welfare and growth, an empathy for their anxieties, and for the terrible sexual responsibilities which biology had placed upon them, all of which made him a unique youth. It was the instinctive realization of this difference in him, contrasted with the exploitative proclivities of his peers, which so attracted girls to him.

As Winston matured in later adolescence, the frenzied heterosexuality faded, and he began to "go steady", with more commitment and involvement each time. There were, of course, a succession of girls, but each love affair seemed deeper and lasted somewhat longer. As the passions of the moment became more urgent, they exerted an increased pressure on both Winston and the girl to feel sincerely that "this was it", and they were truly in love. These emotional upheavals tended to slow down the former rapid turnover of love objects in favor of longer and deeper commitments.

As Winston's affairs grew more serious and single, he wrote more thoughtful and profound poetry, in which the words love and marraige begin to occur, and there is more evidence of some permanent commitment. These behaviors endeared Winston to many girls, for they prized his poetry, since it enhanced their self-esteem. For Winston it was an expression of his talent and love for the current priestess. Some samples:

Come, dearest heart apart; love not the earth,
Nor aught therein, tho pagan nature trace
Through geologic time upon its face

The history of life's triumph and its birth.
The natural values hold no human worth,
And ours in nature have no seemly place:
Man is life's stepchild, yea an orphan race,
Whose verities are dreams, whose Truth is mirth.
Let destiny evolve howe'er it will,
Though prisoners of its power, we have no part
In its blind, tortouous path; our lives fulfill
A second in its scope: soon we depart
Unmissed, as it lives on, — to what? . . . But still
We have each other now . . . Come dearest heart!

* * * * * *

For long I worshipped beauty from afar
   A natural rite a courtly deference,
   To one whose grace and charm and sense
None could deny, no accident could mar.
And then Fate smiled upon my guiding star
   The goddess to a girl transformed, from whence
   Into my arms she came, and thence
Stood I incredulous with joy and awe.
I think whatever destiny hast brought me thee;
   But now fate's part is done; henceforth I swear
Once having known thy love's sincerity
No fate nor fortune be it foul or fair,
   Can loose thee from my love or let thee free, —
For where thou art, dear, my whole heart is there.

Winston found himself at the same time very interested in the entire life cycle of development. Why do people mature at different rates? Why are some people senile at forty and others vital at eighty? Are there stages of development, particularly those beyond adolescent love, and family responsibilities? He read Gandhi's autobiography, among others and was greatly influenced by it. Here was a man who had obviously progressed beyond the householder stage. How had he done so and why? How does one progress from love of self, to love of others, and finally to an altruism, which in the case of St. Francis and Albert Schweitzer extended even to the animals?

By this time, Winston was in college, majoring in English and philology. He continued his strong interest in religion, however, and often attended lectures at the Divinity School. In addition, he continued an interest in physics and tried to make sense out of the universe from that angle. Neither track gave him much closure. He decided to keep a journal notebook and record his thoughts in an effort to make some sense out of the plethora of information which his reading and courses supplied. He instinctively felt that there must be a general solution to the entire problem of existence and that the clarification of mind, which the notebook might supply, might result in a breakthrough. He had learned that the careful inspection of a large amount of miscellaneous data often resulted in the subconscious mind's coming up with a creative pattern of idea which linked up the previously disparate information in a meaningful whole or gestalt. However, he had not reckoned on the form which the reconciliation might take; for the qualities and dimensions of emergence are impossible for the unawakened mind to conceptualize.

In college, Winston met a tall, lovely, and intelligent co-ed named Jean. They quickly fell in love, and grew serious about each other as they found themselves companionable, and with similar interests. It was the first time Winston thought of marriage. Naturally, he wrote impassioned poetry to her:

Sometime you will exclaim: "Why love you me?"
  Yet tho I love you deeply, I'll not say
  'Tis for your face; beauty doth fade away,
And age may soon replace such symmetry.
Your goodness and your grace, your purity
  They all do trace the fineness you display;
  Yet did I love alone for their sweet sway,
Another might excite my sympathy.
Sweetheart of mine, the reason I love you
  Is for your love and for that you are Jean.
  No one can take your place or ever mean
To me the countless sacred things you do.
  Tho all the world be found a painted scene,
What matter, Dear, if still our love be true!

There was an air about Jean which Winston found irresistible. She was serious enough for his deep thoughts, which she understood, and could respond to. But she was also mischievously playful, and full of spritely humor which never failed to enchant him. She had a certain distinguished carriage which made some detractors, mostly other girls, say she was snobby; but she was merely particular and discriminating in her actions and tastes. She had a keen sense of smell, loved the color blue, and adored chocolates, which were bad for her complexion. These were natural failings which Winston found delightful, but he was glad to note that she was much better organized than most co-eds, and seemed to have her head well screwed on.

They were both astonished at the xplosive nature of their love-making. They had started in by being gentle with each other with kissing and fondling, but they quickly discovered that the urgency of their mutual passion soon over—whelmed them. The light petting session would always lead to manual exploration of each other which quickly drove them into a frenzy of love. She would almost immediately be wet for him, and then it was a race to see who could strip off clothes first. Jean was on the pill, so there was no delay for precautions.

Placing her gently on the side of the bed, and standing on the floor facing her he threw her legs back, and thrust himself up into her in a single move. Her joy was such that she thought she should lose consciousness. Then his plunging forays into her deepest being shocked her back to life, and she answered by locking her legs around him in tight embrace, and writhing with joy under his continued thrusts. Faster and faster they came, with deeper and deeper penetration, and his breathing grew hard and noisy. She seemed suspended in time and space, without a will or being of her own, but only his. She wished it would go on for ever, and cried for him never to stop. But at that moment something larger took complete possession of both of them, and their climax came. She could feel him coming, and his excitement triggered her again,, so that they spent together in a whirling ecstasy of delight.

After a short rest, and some kissing and petting, he made her kneel back to him at the side of the bed. He stood behind her, pushing her shoulders down and her buttocks up, and fitting himself into her from the rear. It was a different communication of their bodies, and she felt small, feminine, and helpless in his grasp. Then he seized her wrists from behind, pulling her hands back; and mounting her with some ferocity, he thrust up into her with the most complete penetration she had ever experienced. It seemed as though he had taken complete possession of her. He then began his rhythmic movement, deeper and deeper, each thrust of which seemed to penetrate to her heart and produce a convulsive up-jerk of her body. She had never felt so dominated before; she began to scream with joy at each stroke. Faster and faster they came, and tighter and tighter he held her wrists until the climax overtook them both, and they slumped forward on the bed, still united, but now in peace and contentment.

Naturally and inevitably, this passionate action produced the affective epiphenomena of another sonnet:

Jean my beloved, I need no plumed pen
Ever to tell thy soul my constancy.
All tender ways are mine, my love for thee

Now proudly shines on high before all men.
More o'er it is returned! Thy heart, open
At last to love, sings forth its ecstasy,
Reveals its sweetness and sincerity;
Yet doth subside only to sing again.
Dear girl, as hostages of hope we bear
Under our hearts, desire part satisfied
Now by the glowing flame of love we share —
Companionship, and trust, and mutual pride.
And when I look beyond, dear, thou art there
Nestled within my arms, — my beauteous bride!

★   ★   ★

They were both deliriously happy; it was a season of wine and roses which they wished would go on for ever. The depth of their love produced further evidence of maturity in them both, and provided a strength and bulwark for success in their studies and other activities, rather than detracting from them.

Their affair went along swimmingly. They enjoyed being together whether love-making or not, though that was a constant delight. Jean wanted to get married and raise a family; Winston was enamoured of the idea but held back somewhat because they were only juniors, and it would be nearly two years before he could be on his feet financially.

That summer Jean got a job in a national park, and Winston was saddened at the enforced parting for three months. His worst fears were realized when Jean wrote him a "Dear John" letter. She had fallen in love with a park ranger and they had got married. Winston was desolated, but as usual even this emotion brought on a poem:

Within an unseen corner of my heart
Far from the tumult which each work day knows,
There lay a magic world thus set apart
Where I might find diversion and repose.

Within that realm of fancy for it was
Freshening and fleet as ever morning dew,
There lay a cynic's romance, all because
The life and breath of romance moved in you.

And oft discouraged by the daily round
I sought the secret bliss of my domain,
And there, with you as guide, redemption found;

My soul refilled; my vision came again.

And now 'tis done, for as the breaking day
Doth with her shining lamp the dewdrops steal,
So broadening circumstance takes you away,
And bids me drop illusion for the real.

I have no fault to find with restless fate;
I have no cry to make against the sun;
I can but linger o'er a vanished state
And rightly value romance now 'tis done.

It took Winston some time to regain his equinamity after this jolt. First he blamed the whole female sex for being frail and inconstant. But he finally realized that it was not a psychological put-down to let fester, but a simple case of a girl who was emotionally and physically ready for love and marriage, and who could not restrain herself from jumping at the first good chance. His only miscue, if indeed it was one, was in not marrying her at once. This rationalization helped him cognitively, but affectively the wound still bled. If love could hurt him this much, clearly he would find it hard to fall so completely in love again. He expressed his readjustment of feelings as follows:

When from the long day's grind and drudgery,
When hopes and bosom friends have traitors played,
When all life's purpose seems of carrion made,
When all the world is harsh and out of key.
And dark dispair and discord tempts my thought
To spurn its trust and cast away its soul
For patience has no balm and faith no goal,
And all this wide world's uses are as naught, —
Why then upon a lonely hill at night and free
I watch the crystal-shaped stars that slide
Like a great host of ancient pagentry
Across the naked heavens slowly glide;
Then grace and beauty bring my strength amain,
And I arise calm and refreshed again.

★   ★   ★

One night Winston had a particularly vivid dream. It started out in a typically sexual fashion. He was with a beautiful young girl in a

102

diaphanous gown which partly revealed her delectable figure. he started to embrace her; but although complacent, and not forbidding, she drew away from him. He pursued her, took her in his arms, and somehow removed her bodice, revealing a pair of small, but beautifully formed breasts. Emboldened, he began to remove more of her clothing, which seemed to come off in layers, next revealing her firm belly and soft navel. Visibly impassioned by these sight, he stripped off her last shreds of clothing but was struck dumb with wonderment; she had no genitalia at all. Seeing his surprise, she nodded to him lovingly, putting her finger over her mouth, and rose gently upward, making him understand that she was an angelic being. Surprisingly, he was not frustrated, but rather awed at the sight, which somehow signified some sort of transcendence, some more than earthly favor to be bestowed upon him. The dream had been very vivid, and he thought about its meaning a good deal.

★ ★ ★

Because of an interest in astronomy, Winston had gained the confidence of the professor in charge and was on occasion rewarded by being allowed to use the small 8″ telescope by himself. One moonless night he was on duty — it was still rather early, before midnight — and he was alone in the small observatory, which was dark except for a few footlights so that one could better see the heavens. He had been looking through the glass at the moons of Jupiter when suddenly one of them occulted behind the planet. He stopped to sit down and rest. What happened next is best told in his own words as he recorded it in his journal:

[1]"All of a sudden something amazing happened to me. My hair stood on end, my fingers pricked, my spine tingled, and there was a lump in my stomach; a curtain of red seemed to fall before my eyes.[1] [2]As though coming from another realm, a startling but marvelous experience blazed forth in my consciousness. It was as if someone had intoned 'Open Sesame' to roll back the guardian stone from the hidden treasure house.[2] [3]Something invisible had been drawn across the sky transforming the world about me into a kind of tent of concentrated and enhanced significance. What had been merely an outside became an inside. The objective was transformed somehow into the subjective, which was experienced as "mine" but on a level where the word had no further personal significance, for 'I' was no longer the familiar ego.[3]

[4]I felt myself going, losing myself. Then I was terrified, but with a strange sweet terror. I was losing my consciousness — my identty — but I was powerless to help myself.[4] [5]Panic-struck, thinking I was having some kind of attack, I leaned forward to steady myself, as the world seemed to rock about me.[5] [6]I could not separate the spiritual and the physical of that

moment. My physical body went through the experience of a disappearance in spiritual light. All separate lines in the front of phenomena became plastic and relaxed. I was one with God, Love, the Universe, arrived at last face-to-face with myself. I was sensible of peculiar moral and mental disturbances and readjustments. There was a sense of immediacy about it all, and abolute and indissoluble unity of all the energies in my being into one central all-living force.[6]

[4]I was seeing and comprehending the sublime meaning of all things, the reasons for all that which before had been hidden and dark. The great truth that life is a spiritual evolution, that this life is but a passing phase in the soul's progression, that all is well and will be well, burst upon my astonished vision with overwhelming grandeur. And still the splendor increased. Presently what seemed to be a swift oncoming tidal wave of splendor and glory ineffable came down upon me, engulfing me completely and swallowing me up in its overwhelming beauty and majesty.[4]

[4]Now came a period of rapture so intense that the universe seemed to stand still as if amazed by the unutterable majesty of the spectacle. Only One is all the universe. The all-loving, the perfect One. The Monad. The perfect Wisdom, Truth, Love and Purity. And with this rapture came insight. In that same wonderful moment of what might be called supernal bliss came illumination. For I saw with intense inward vision the very atoms and molecules of which seemingly the universe is composed, rearranging themselves in an everlasting dance of continuous life as the cosmos passes from order to increasing order. With joy I saw that there was no break in the chain — not a link left out — everything in its proper place and time, like one gigantic symphony. World, systems, galaxies, all blended into one harmonious and plenary whole.[4]

[3]I remember saying to myself, 'So it's like this; now I know what Heaven is like; now I know what they mean in church.' The words of the 23rd Psalm came into my head and I began repeating them,[3] with tears of joy streaming down my face. The glimpse of that sacred second into the depths of immortality left no doubt nor qualification. I had seen the byss and the abyss, myself. [7]I was utterly amazed. Is this the answer to the mystery of Life? But it is too simple; I always knew it — it is like remembering an old forgotten secret — like coming home — I am not I, not the I I thought.[7]

There is no death — peace passing understanding, yet how unworthy am I of this vision. I thought of the lines from Bishop Bosquanet: [8]And now we are saved absolutely, we need not say from what; we are at home in the universe, and there is nothing that can ever make us afraid again.' "[8]

How long he was in this state Winston did not know. He gradually came to himself, and very slowly shut up the place and walked back to his dormitory. He realized that something like a watershed had occurred in his life. But his mind was too full to think further, and he fell into a deep and comforting sleep.

Somehow the mystical experience had put to rest some conflicts and resolved others; his mind was now calm. When he awoke, he had formulated several propositions. First, the experience was not just nominal; it had some point and significance; his job was to find out what. Second, there must be a way to acquire this esoteric knowledge, which his college studies had thus far failed to supply; third, this way might well be, as was the vision, a product of interior insight and revelation, rather than external study.

He needed a method for producing this interior wisdom at will. He had always been good at creative revery. It seemed to him that he would prepare to write in his journal a dialog between himself and various wisdom figures of the past. His hypothesis was that just as his subconscious mind could supply creative ideas of his own, it could also supply the creative ideas of others since they all must come from some common interior source. He hoped to learn consciously by this method what the subconscious already knew and by so bringing the conscious and subconscious into accordance to integrate himself, or, in an old phraseology, to ground himself.

One night several months after the first dream, Winston had another of the same urgency and vividness. He was riding a white horse through the sky pursuing a group of flying nymphs, when suddenly the horse was killed as if by a stroke and Winston plunged downward into the sea. He realized that he was drowning and gave himself up for lost. The world began to spin around him and he entered a tunnel; at the other end of it was a shaft of light. As he hurtled through the tunnel the light became a living Presence. Winston found himself spreadeagled at its feet. Then an amazing thing happened. The Light somehow reached forth and gathered the seminal fluid from him; then the Light cast forth some of these seeds and they entered Winston's body causing a jolt of electricity all the way up his spine. The Light cast forth the remainder of the seed, and they became little twinkling stars, which arranged themselves into a shining chariot, glistening with brilliance. It was given to Winston to understand that he should enter the chariot and be transported to an ideal place, where both mind and body are refreshed. All this was accomplished without any fear or dread on Winston's part. He entered the chariot and it swiftly bore him to that other realm, where he was instructed by an old and wise man. The new knowledge was very welcome to Winston. Then the chariot brought him back, and he woke up without being able to remember anything of what had been taught him in this amazing fashion. Nevertheless the dream had a remarkable impact on him, and he instinctively realized that it meant some kind of turning point in his life.

Gradually Winston recalled what the wise man had told him. His seminal fluid was too precious to waste in ejaculation. Instead it should be conserved, and absorbed internally, wherein it conferred psychic powers, starting with creativity and healing. Without this continence, such powers were impossible. However, this teaching did not mean that sex was evil, for it was obviously necessary for the continuance of the race. The sexual power was but one outlet — (and the lowest at that) — of pranic energy, which could also be expressed in these higher ways. For other more ordinary men it might be different, but for him, because of his unique abilities, a transcendence of the energy outlet needed to be made if he were to fit himself for his mission on earth. Like every other ability given to man, sexual energy was to be used wisely and with attention to its higher rather than its lower potential.

This teaching resulted in an attitude on Winston's part which in no way condemned sexual activity, nor consigned him to strict and unremitting continence. It was more like the building of a dam across a flowing river. If the dam did not let through some water, it would be overtaxed and eventually destroyed; but the dam performs the useful function of diverting some water into irrigation canals and of using the rest to turn electrical dynamos. This insight gave Winston a new and less guilt-ridden approach to sex in all its forms. He now saw it just another developmental task which one is first overwhelmed by, then which one is involved in, and finally, one which surmounts and is able to look at objectively.

About this time, Winston had another dream or vision. He tells about it in his own words from his journal:

[9]"I saw (I cannot say I dreamed, for it was quite different from dreaming since I was seated on the side of my bed) a beautiful angelic pure being, and myself standing along-side of her, feeling a most heavenly pure joy. And it was as if . . . our bodies were luminous, and they gave forth a moonlight glow, which I felt sprung from the joy we experienced in being together. We were unclothed, pure, and unconscious of everything but love and joy; and I felt as if we had always been together and that our motions, actions, feelings and thoughts came from one center. And when I looked toward her, I saw no bold outline of form, but an angelic something I cannot describe save in angelic shape and image. This experience has left such an indelible impression upon my mind that for sometime afterwards, I continued to feel the same influence, and do so now, so that the actual world around me has lost its hold . . . For I am still charmed by that influence, and I am conscious that if

I should accept anything else in its place, I should lose the very life and love which is the only existence wherein I wish to live."[9]

Needless to say, these dreams and thoughts created a great deal of controversy in Winston's mind. He was a powerfully sexed young man, at the height of his prowess, and yet he was evidently being asked to give up this level of expression for something higher. The "something higher" clearly involved artistic creativity, for Winston found himself writing verse as he never had written before. But this new power also appeared to embrace psychic and healing capacities which were at this time ill-defined, but which he was compelled to explore.

Nowhere is this metamorphosis shown better than in Winston's poetry of this period. Three samples in sequence of his developmental escalation illustrate this change perfectly:

AN IDEAL FOR WINSTON

HE who is strong and who enduring stands
Alone and friendless through the bitter fight,
Who conquers self with service, wrong with right,
Who will not flinch nor flee when Truth demands,
Whose Purity is as the strength of ten,
Whose heart is brave and true, whose aim is high,
Whose matchless spirit dares to do or die,
Whose strength brings out the good in other men,
He will endure and though he fall amain,
(He walks by faith and not by temporal sight)
Yet will arise and at his task again,
Persist with vigor and redoubled might,
Till finally from a world of War and Pain,
He goes to Victory and Eternal Light.

★ ★ ★

METAMORPHOSIS

[10]*El Toro, waking, rises from his bed,*
Gathers full strength and with deliberate tread
Ambles into the gleaming, magic stall —
Debates and contemplates the waterfall —
Then, dares the plunge, his daily morning rite.

Beneath the streaming fall which pours and crashes —

Unseen, the powerful figure strives and thrashes —
His hearty bellow transforms to mighty roar —
And Leo claims identity over Tor'.

Asserting all his claims in sounds and stances
Proud lion from the showering falls now prances.
Majestically his Kingdom he entrances
With magical masks of lather and sly glances.
With morning ritual his vanity he enhances.

And when his labor's done to satisfaction,
He turns — without the slightest of distraction,
And unaware of rays of light's refraction,
He in that turning has surrendered to
The essence of a spell that strips him true.

Just as one golden sunbeam gilds the morn,
And falls on him, a mantle to adorn —
Transforms, imbues him with a grace new born,
So Leo, now his lofty rank's forsworn,
Defers. And from the quiet mist — all mystery shorn —
Out steps, untamed, the rare and fabled Unicorn.[10]

★   ★   ★

LIBERATION

Imprisoned thricely by the walls
Of time, space and personage,
When shall we heed the voice that calls
To tell us of our lineage?

It rises silent as a spring
Within the quiet of the mind;
It is a different sort of thing;
It bids us leave the world behind.

In time's cocoon we swing asleep, —
Perchance a lucid dream tonight
To will begone the pupal deep
And wing the butterfly aflight.

Arise my soul and seek thee now

The glory of the noumenon;
For thou art That, and That art thou;
So from thy fetters hence begone.

Man is not dust; he comes afar
And recognizes not his home.
Our sun is but the morning star
To that celestial dawn to come.

Oh Spirit, that has made us bold
To think such thoughts in lieu of Thee,
Make manifest in men untold
This avenue to liberty.

★   ★   ★

There is an occult saying: "When the pupil is ready, the master appears." This development happened for Winston on the occasion when, on impulse, he heard a visiting guru lecture on transpersonal matters at the University. The swami had once been a Harvard physics professor, but had given up his Western training, and had embraced a Hindu name and religion after an extensive discipleship in India with a noted Vedanta leader. He then returned to America and established an ashram in Oregon. The speech riveted Winston's attention, and after a brief talk with the guru, he felt himself drawn to join the ashram. He wished to undertake the mind-expansion which it promised, especially as it offered a procedure devoid of the usual sectarian or creedal strictures, and embraced a compatibility with scientific intellectualism.

In taking this definitive step, Winston was not sure whether his creative talents would blossom in poetry, prose or healing, but he sensed that to perfect them would require the quiet and coherence which such training would develop. The withdrawal would allow him time to find in himself the medium in which his return would be couched. So we leave Winston not yet twenty-five, in process of making this transformation, confident that in whatever way the creative talents within him emerge, they will be of use and benefit not only to himself but to humanity as well.

9 — WINSTON

[1]Laski (1962:418) quoting Richard Church.
[2]Gowan (1974:114) quoting J. Blofeld *The Tantric Mysticism of Tibet.*
[3]Happold (1963:130) quoting M. Isherwood, *The Root of the Matter.*

[4]Bucke (1901:326) quoting C.M.C.

[5]Citation lost.

[6]Bucke (1901:346) quoting Horace Traubel.

[7]Happold (1963:133) quoting Warner Allen *The Timeless Moment*.

[8]Happold (1963:131) quoting Vera Brittain *Testament of Youth* quoting Bishop Bosanquet.

[9]Graef (1962:67) quoting the vision of Thomas Hecker in Hecker's own words.

[10]An unpublished poem by Betty Hobbs.

CHAPTER 10
Anthony

The straitjacket was curtailing his breathing, and Anthony woke up with a start. The white padded room without furniture of any kind stared him in the face. He blinked a bit uncomprehendingly at first, and tried to recollect how he had come to this. Then he remembered the sound and the fury, the terrors and the horrors. To banish these goblins from his mind he forced himself to think of long-forgotten happier days — of his childhood and youth and its erstwhile peaceful scenes.[1]

Tony recalled growing up in Christchurch, New Zealand, in a little house off Gloucester St., just over the bridge, about halfway between Cathedral Square and the University of Canterbury. He was the only child of somewhat older parents, who had lavished all their love and affection on him. He father had been reared on a sheep station in the middle of the North Island, but, after agricultural school, had decided on trade instead of sheep-raising, and had become a successful butcher. He had met Tony's mother when she was a student at the Teacher Training College at Palmerston North, and, when she got a job teaching at Christchurch, he had followed her to the South Island where they were married and set up housekeeping.

As a child Tony loved to wander along the banks of the beautiful river Avon, gathering plants and flowers, and pressing them into his special book for that purpose. He used to contemplate with fascination the marble statue to the doomed antarctic explorer, Scott, which stood beside the Gloucester Street bridge, (for Scott had set out from Christchurch on his ill-fated trip to the South Pole), and he used to repeat its brave sentiment: "Let them know that Englishmen in this century can die as bravely as in the past." Then he would go down to the water and feed the ducks, or walk over to the great park and look for exotic plants.

He remembered those special Sunday afternoons when his parents would take him to the great university hall for a musicale, and he would regard with admiration the large picture of Lord Rutherford, the famous

111

scientist and Canterbury's most distinguished graduate, hanging high on the front wall behind the orchestra. Then afterwards his father would show him the simple polished brass plate on the side wall which merely said: RUTHERFORD, then underneath in Latin "To inquire into the original order of things." There was something magnificent about its simplicity, as if the single surname was quite enough for recognition around the world. His father never tired of pointing out to Anthony that here in these two monuments were exemplified the two great virtues of man, — bravery and intelligence. So Tony's childhood, full of simle pleasures, passed peacefully and uneventfully, with no hint of the trouble which was to befall him at adolescence.

The first inkling of difficulty came at the end of his fourth form in the local preparatory school. The headmaster advised his father that Tony's grades were not entirely strong enough to risk examination at Canterbury, where there was great competition. He suggested that Tony transfer to St. Barnabas Academy at Wellington and seek to enter Massey College at Palmerston North. With some reluctance the parents pooled their resources, and sent Tony to St. Barnabas. He was admonished to study harder, which he did, and was ultimately successful at matriculating at the somewhat less difficult institution.

He was offered a job that summer at a hotel in the thermal area of Rotorura in the North Island of New Zealand, and anxious to prove his independence as well as to earn some extra funds for his college expenses, he eagerly accepted. But while there, another untoward event happened, which, though he had become attracted to girls, very considerably colored his relationship with them thereafter.

One hot summer night he had taken a girl he rather liked to the movies. On coming out they were surprised at how warm it was. He suggested they get some air by going to the cove where there was a beautiful beach, and she was agreeable. When they got there the water was so warm, and the mooonlight on it so inviting, that on a sudden impulse they decided to go swimming. They waded into the soft water, she with only her panties on, and he naked. In the water, after swimming a bit she came to him, and he kissed her lips, then holding her tighter cupped her firm breasts with his hands. She sighed with passion, and clung to him altogether, wrapping her legs around his body, and thereby giving him a hard erection. He was ashamed, but she did not seem disturbed, and indicated that she wanted to go up on the beach, so he carried her there and lay her down on the sand. She motioned him to come over her, and this time he kissed her breast with rising ardor. She was visibly impassioned, and quickly reaching out took his penis in hand and began to squeeze it gently. He was on top of her now, but before he could remove her panties and spread her legs for full coition, to his horror

112

and amazement he found himself in the grip of a convulsive ejaculation which sprayed semen all over her upper body from neck to navel. She let go of him immediately, but he continued the convulsive jerking until he had spent the last of the seminal fluid on her belly.

She cried out "Why did you do that?" and rose, dashing into the lake to cleanse herself. He had never been so ashamed and embarrassed in his whole life.

They dressed quickly, and he took her home. She said little, but he knew he was done for. She would never go out with him again. For that matter he would never dare ask her.

It was his last explicit experience with a girl. How could he ever face one again? It was one thing not to know what the girl would do, but not to know what he himself would do was too much anxiety to bear. Even masturbation was no consolation, for the squirting semen reminded him again and again of that dreadful hour.

Anthony's further trouble had begun in a seemingly quiet way. Just before going away to college he had told his parents at breakfast of a strange compelling dream. A dark, tall and rather forbidding beautiful woman had appeared to him in this dream, and offered herself to him if he would be her slave. He had refused and she had cursed him and told him that he would be haunted by the furies she would unleash upon him. Anthony seemed genuinely disturbed by this nightmare, for it apparently had seemed very real to him at the time. He described it vividly to his parents. His mother was alarmed, but his father confided to her later that it was probably nothing more than a veiled sexual dream, which should be a welcome sign, since it showed that their son was fighting carnal temptations, natural at his age. Anthony, however, had no such easy explanation. He felt that the dream was a supernatural omen.

Nothing else untoward occurred during the short remainder of his visit home, and late in February he left for the fall term at Massey. Palmerston North is a railroad junction and agricultural depot for a large and fertile plain in the middle of the North Island. Naturally, Massey College was mainly agricultural in emphasis, though other majors had gradually been added. The buildings stood on a prominent bluff above the Manawatu River just west of town, and the grounds were beautifully landscaped with many exotic shrubs and trees. The buildings were mainly British colonial, with high ceilings, wide hallways, and large windows, prevalent before the advent of air conditioning. There were many outhouse buildings where animal husbandry was taught, and a large grain and legume experimental station. There were herds of cows and sheep grazing on the flood plain below.

The town was a natural mecca for farmers and their markets. The railroad tracks ran straight down the main street, and completely tied up the town square when the trains stopped to let off passengers from Wellington or to take up those bound for Auckland. It was a busy, bustling county seat, made pleasant by the generous and felicitous nature of the inhabitants. Anthony took a small room in a nearby rooming house and bicycled each morning the mile or so to classes. Life for him seemed once again to be settling into a comfortable and stable pattern.

All went well for a short time, and then Tony's troubles started again. The landlady ordered him out; she was reluctant to give a reason, but upon being pressed said it was because he had noisy nightmares during which he uttered bloodcurdling screams, and once or twice he had been found walking in his sleep. Anthony applied for a space in the residential college, and since there was a vacancy he was quickly settled in.

Eight weeks passed uneventfully and all seemed well, when one evening his parents got a trunk call from the university dean. Since his father had studied animal husbandry at Massey and was a respected alumnus, the conversation was informal. "I'm sorry to tell you," said the dean, "We've had some problems with Tony; I'm wondering if you could come up tomorrow to confer with me about him." Aware that this was no ordinary summons, but unable to get more specifics from the dean on the phone, Anthony's father came up on the morning Electra next day. From the dean's reticence he expected that Tony had become involved in a sexual situation of some sort.

He went directly to the dean's office. His rather shaken son was waiting for him in the anteroom, as was Dr. Hayden, the school physician. They were quickly ushered into the inner office, but Tony was asked to stay behind. After the usual pleasantries, the dean got straight to the point.

"I'm very sorry to bring you here at such short notice, but Tony has been behaving peculiarly, and we feel that since it may be the onset of some kind of nervous breakdown, perhaps it might be best for you to take him out of college for a semester to rest up and regain his composure. "Let me tell you of some of the facts about Tony which have been reported to me. About two weeks ago Tony created a mild disturbance by going to the girls' dormitory in his night clothes and robe about midnight and waking up the matron. He then told her in a rather wild fashion that they had been accusing him of having raped all the girls on the third floor, but it was not true, he had never been on the third floor. Alarmed, she called the police and he willingly went with them to the stationhouse and again protested his innocence of the rape charges. There had, in fact, been no attacks on the girls, and the entire thing seemed to be a figment of Tony's imagination.

"Then Dr. Spencer of the English Department brought me a theme which Tony had turned in." said the dean. "Dr. Spencer said the contents alarmed him, and he felt that he should not take the responsibiliy of withholding them from a higher official. I have the paper here, and I will show it to you as soon as I finish. Third, last Sunday, Tony disrupted a vesper service by suddenly appearing in the congregation and loudly proclaiming that they were all sinners, that judgment day with the awful wrath of God was coming shortly, and that he was willing to sacrifice his life to atone for the sins of all. Needless to say, this created considerable stir and Tony received a lot of opprobrious attention from the student body."

★ ★ ★

Letter to God:
Almighty and Awful Master of the Universe: I denounce myself as a miserable sinner. I am in peril of death and condemnation to everlasting hellfire. But in the great disaster which Thy righteous wrath shall spread on us for our heinous sins, I offer myself as a willing sacrifice for the sins of others. I cannot stand Thy accusing voices any longer. They charge me with dreadful sins too vile to mention, fornication, bestiality and all other forms of carnal lewdness. They read my mind and prevent me from carrying out my best resolves. They have poisoned my food so that I am in fear of daily death. Electric currents shoot through my body from head to toe, down my spine, making my penis tingle, and thence down my legs and out my feet. They know that I am at the apex of good effort and resolve, and therefore they attack me at my weakness so that I may die a sinner and be confined to hell forever. They force me to masturbate, while they place fantasies of alluring but wicked female bodies in my mind to taunt and to harass me. They have incapacitated me to the extent that I cannot do what I would to obey Thy commands, and I unwillingly sin against Thee while I am terrified at the awful punishment such sinning will bring. Oh, God, forgive me for these dreadful faults and take away my sin and suffering. Admit me to Thy peace and have mercy upon me a most miserable sinner.

★ ★ ★

After perusing the letter, and somewhat shaken by its contents, Tony's father turned to the dean. The dean went on. "We want to handle this unfortunate situation in the best possible way. This is not a usual disciplinary matter. It seems to be more of a medical problem. That is why

I have asked Dr. Hayden to join us here for his diagnosis and advice."

"It is a little early to make an accurate diagnosis in Tony's case," Dr. Hayden opined. "It may be a sexual aberration, though I discount that concept. It seems more likely to be a nervous breakdown of some sort, though further undefined. It could be the beginning of something far more serious, namely *dementia praecox,* a mental disease much like schizophrenia which seems to attack young men for reasons which are not obvious. In any case, the boy needs a rest without any pressure for at least a semester. It would be far better to give him a medical leave now and wipe the semester clean than to let him go on to failure and/or academic or disciplinary probation. Then, of course, when he is better, he could come back with a clean record."

"Obviously," said the dean, "We cannot let Tony stay under these conditions. And that is why I phoned you to come. Had I written, it would have gone into his file. You can withdraw him upon medical advice without any further penalty and nothing more will go into his record."

There was nothing to do, of course, except follow the dean's advice, so Tony's father took Tony home. They took the afternoon train to Wellington, got berths on the overnight boat to Lyellton and arrived from the boat train at Christchurch depot the next morning. Tony was quiet and subdued during the trip, but offered no explanation, and his father was too worried and concerned to press him further. His parents felt that home environment, home cooking and some tender loving care, with no responsibilities, might be enough to bring him to his senses again, and their efforts seemed justified the first week or so.

But about ten days later his father and mother were roused from their bed about 3:00 A.M. by furious knocking at the front door. It was the police; Tony had been picked up running naked around Christchurch square, and trying to break into the Cathedral. He was very incoherent, but his ultimate explanation was that the Devil was after him, and that he wanted to save himself by taking refuge in the sanctuary. Once again Tony, in a comatose state was brought home, and a doctor was called who sedated him. This time, the doctor had some severe advice for the parents. "I'm sorry to have to tell you, but Tony will have to be committed for an indefinite time, in the local psychiatric hospital where he can get treatment for this mental disturbance. It is impossible to predict how long that will take. Sometimes cases of this type are chronic and go on for years; in other instances they lead up to a climax, and then there is some chance of total remission. If that should be the case, you must steel yourselves to find Tony much worse soon, and that is why he needs to be confined."

Tony was duly admitted in a few days time, and, true to the doctor's prediction, he continued to have more and more severe periodic seizures; during some of these he became violent, and it was necesary to use restraints, and to place him in a special cell. He began to smell like an animal and to snort and growl like one. Whatever was possessing him seemed inhuman and demonic. For Tony it was a real green-eyed demon who would come at these times and sit on his back. He would direct other minions to devour Tony's flesh, so that only the bones were left, and Tony would find himself as a skeleton, on a barren, dark, waterless plain. This plain was an evil fearful place, where malignant shapes wandered, some palpable, and some invisible, except for two eyes which always seemed to accuse Tony of unheard-of but dreadful crimes. Then there were the lights; not all the lights were the same. Some were small and flickering, and often of different colors, in which blue and yellow predominated. Others were larger and egg-shaped, some being much bigger. Tony was drawn to these, but they always escaped his approach. Occasionally there was an unusual one with two white plumes of light projecting from an oval aura. Tony instinctively realized that these lights represented people, or rather the trace of people in this strange land of magic and mystery, so dark and foreboding. The whole experience gave him that sick-to-the-stomach panicky feeling he had on previous occasions when he had got into trouble. These waking nightmares seemed real to Tony as if everything good, light and beautiful were somehow distorted and changed into something ugly, dark and sinister. Even when all his fears of some dreadful catastrophe happening proved groundless, the ordeal left him sick and exhausted. Fortunately, the drugs the doctor gave him helped to sedate him and to that extent banish some of these interior horrors, and he slept in a catatonic stupor at such times, grateful for the respite from this living hell.

★　★　★

He was standing in front of a very large temple building with great brass doors at least two stories high. He knocked, and the doors slowly swung open. Within was a vast hall, with priests and hierophants; at the other end of which, seated on a golden upraised dias, was an enormous nude goddess. Her breasts were firm, and her body beautiful, but there was something dreadful about her eyes which seemed to strike fire. "Approach, stranger," the goddess intoned, "Are you the man who will impregnate me with child?" Because of their disparity in size, it was obvious that this would be impossible. He began to be afraid. The goddess commanded, "Strip off his clothes." and a trice he was nude. "He is wanting," she said, and as if to verify her words, his masculinity shriveled to nothing. "Then he shall pay the price," exclaimed the goddess. "Thrust him head first into my womb, that he may suffocate there and so engender my child." Hot oil was poured on Tony, and despite his screams they made ready for this awful fate. But suddenly he evaded their clutches and dashed out of the building. "After him! After him!" screamed the goddess. "Bring him back to me dead or alive."

Tony ran into the woods, where they could not find him; but suddenly all the foliage shriveled and disappeared, so that he could easily be spotted in the denuded forest. "After him! After him!" was the cry. He spurted on in panic and fear. Then the goddess made everything at an angle, so that he and his pursuers were running on the slant; still they did not catch him. Then the goddess began to shorten his stature, so that his strides became less. In order to make up for this disadvantage, he gradually began to discard various parts of his body, his arms, his flesh, even some of his bones, until he was just a skeleton; finally his tormentors caught up with him. "Let us boil his bones," they said, "and eat them first; thus we shall be refreshed, and better able to bring back the remains to the temple." A cauldron was brought and Tony was dumped into it. "Help me, help me," he begged. And then he woke up.

It was hard to say if these waking nightmares were dreams or not; Tony was merely grateful to find himself safe from the horrors of a few moments ago. He was lying in an all-white padded cell with absolutely no furniture — indeed, nothing except a pillow. There were not even any power points, so that he could not electrocute himself. At one end of the cell was a door, also white, and barely distinguishable from the rest; it was also padded except for a one foot square window to the outside. The room was softly lit.

An attendant dressed in white entered. "Do you want to go to the bathroom?" he asked. "You've been having a bad time, and we had to put you in here for a while. The doctor will come with something to help you sleep, so maybe now we better get the bathroom taken care of."

Tony's mouth was dry. He wanted water or some kind of drink. "You can have some in the bathroom," the attendant said. They went and returned; the doctor came and gave Tony an injection. Tony felt sleepy and laid down on the padding. The room was warm enough so that he did not require a blanket over his pajamas. How long he slept, he did not know, but when he awakened, he was hungry and thirsty.

The waking and sleeping horrors came and went, like showers during an extended atmospheric low. When they were not upon him, Tony, though depressed, was quite rational and while very ashamed to have any friend or relative see him in this plight, could recognize them and talk more or less rationally. But he was obsessed by fear that at any moment, the horrors might return. Fortunately, the tranquilizing medicine the doctor administered seemed to be taking effect, at least for the time being.

But these episodes of hallucinating nightmares occurred with increasing regularity and terror. In one of them, Tony found himself, whether awake or dreaming, he could never remember, in what he had learned to call the "never-never" land. It was a dark dry plain of a landscape, with little adornment or relief, lit only by tiny white lights which glided to and fro. There was nothing else there except these lights, which flittered hither and yon in a forbidding and threatening darkness. Furthermore, as in most of his nightmares, there were invisible entities, demons, they seemed, which can seize hold of one. While watching this strange panorama, Tony felt himself suddenly seized, as if from behind, by one of these evil forces. It wrestled him to the ground, and completely overpowered him, choking off his breathing, so that in his extremity he cried out to God to save him from death.

Immediately, the nightmare vanished, and Tony, adrip with sweat and tears, was immured in a rosy glow. He heard God's voice from inside him say, "My grace is enough for thee." For some unexplainable reason these simple words had an enormous effect on Tony, for they seemed to free him from the panic-fear of this dark and sinister nightmare, and to replace that dread and horror with love, joy and assurance. At the same time he felt inwardly healed of his illness, and in complete certainty of the love and presence of God. His sense of sin dropped away, and he felt no more compunctions about death. How long he remained in this state, he did not know.

Sometime later, one of the nurses found him kneeling, praying and crying in an attitude of prayer.

"Are you all right?" she queried. "Why are you crying?"

"Because God has granted me His grace," Tony replied. "He has forgiven me as a sinner. He has taken my sickness away, and has restored me to health."

The nurse shook her head. "You have had another bad spell, and you need to rest in bed." she stated, leading him there by the hand.

"But I am well; I am whole; I am free." Tony responded. "I can go home now and resume my studies. Please call my father and ask him to come and get me."

★ ★ ★

Tony was right; he was over it, although it took a little time for the hospital to decide he was fit to be released. Within the week his father was summoned to take him home. But he was far from the same person he had been before. During his convalescence he showed a strong interest in healing, and in folk medicine, and when he was well enough to travel he begged his parents to let him go to Rotorura, where, besides taking the thermal baths, he wanted to talk with a Maori medicine man whose acquaintance he had made in the summer he worked there. It was

January, and school would not be in session until March, so they let him go.

Tony got the old Maori to show him the natural herbs the Maori used for curing disease, and when he returned to Massey in March he majored in botany, with special attention to native plants and herbs. He spent a couple of years there, but left before graduation, and settled down in the South Island as a herbalist. It was some time before he could support himself, but his parents were overjoyed that he had become useful and happy.

It would be idle to pretend that Tony had returned to live a normal life. The mark of the shaman was on him, for he still had occasional seizures and trances; but he seemed more in control of these than formerly, and he was not afraid. He found himself a little hut on the edge of the bush, some distance from town, and lived the life of a bachelor and hermit, apparently never needing nor seeking the company of women. He sold herbs, some of which he grew and the rest of which he gathered from the forest. He also began to acquire a reputation as a healer. He could relieve back pain by a touch of his hands. He became a familiar figure in Christchurch in his itinerant wanderings peddling herbs and nostrums, and he developed a steady clientele who swore by his concoctions. He seemed much more at home with the Maori than with his own people, and frequently visited them. Above all, he was a gentle and peaceable naturalist, whose knowledge of forest lore and flora often resulted in his being employed as a guide with occasional lectures on native plants.

In short, Tony became successful at what he valued, and hence useful to a society which he stood outside of, but which prized him, nevertheless, for his healing arts.

10 — ANTHONY

¹This story has been constructed so as to be a classic example of "shaman's sickness" or *dementia praecox*. For further to this subject see Boisen 1936.

CHAPTER 11
Miss Tennoyer

My name is Almeda Tennoyer and I was brought up on a farm in the eastern townships of Canada, south of Sherbrooke, and near to the watershed between the St. Lawrence basin and the New England rivers. Our large farm was worked mainly for growing hay and raising beef, although on the back acres there was a little hardwood, mostly maple. I was the only daughter of an English gentleman farmer whose forebears had been traced back to the Conquest. My mother was a scion of a well-to-do and very pious family who lived across the line in Vermont. Both she and my father had been but indifferently educated, but they were very strong church people, and I went to Sunday School every Sunday.[1]

Things were very simple in those pre World War I years. Folks traveled in buggies, as autos were virtually unknown. When five, I remember an outing to Sawyerville where I saw to my amazement my first railroad train and was scared to death by the noise, smoke and steam of the engine. In the winter the roads were full of snow and ice, so that sometimes the horses had a hard time of it, and we used to use pungs and sleighs. The boys would hook a ride on the large pung skates but I was not allowed to. The turn of the seasons dominated our lives. Spring brought mud, then birds, then flowers, then new baby animals, which we children made pets of. It was summer, however, that I liked best, with its long, lazy days and lingering twilights, often succeeded at night by Northern Lights. I would often take a lunch up to the hill, alternately looking out on the blue mountains in the far distance where the air always seemed clearer and searching in the grass for little blueberries to spice the meal.

Fall was the time for harvest and bounties of food and festivities. The trees wore their brightest colors, and the maples especially blushed red and gold. Those were simple days, with much work around the house and farm. Since we made almost everything we used, from soap to cheese, a visit by an itinerant tinsmith or knife-sharpener was a rare excitement.

Despite the simple life we led, there were many events to enjoy. In the winter there were sleigh rides, and the inevitable "kiss-me-quicks" — those places, generally over a brook, where the snow had melted into a depression which often dipped the sleigh below the snow level of the shoulders, especially if there were drifts. I can still remember the jingling bells of the sleighs amid the cold starlight and our hands nestled in muffs and mittens and the coarse horsehair lap robe, which always smelled of the tack room. Then there were the sugaring off parties with the hot sugar on snow, fresh from the boiling-down kettle, out by the little smoke cabin which served as the focus of the sap collecting in February and March. The maple candy was so good and sweet it had to be washed down with vinegar to restore one's taste. Occasionally we would give a lump of it to the dog and then clamp his jaws shut over it; and then we'd dissolve in laughter as the poor canine tried to lick it away before he could open his mouth again.

In the spring there were quilting bees and other church sociables (most often for the benefit of the Missionary society) with some relaxation in discipline and the strict bed-time hours so that they were always a treat for us children.

Then there were the June strawberry festivals, with their delicious wild and tame berries crushed either in real, thick cream or even better (if the ice was plentiful) in real home-made ice cream enough to send even a saint to bed with distended stomach.

In the summer there was the smell of new mown hay, and the raker and the tedder which I sometimes got to ride. The men dried and gathered the new hay, hoping to cure it in the fitful sunshine and get it safely indoors before the next shower came along and spoiled it dark. Everyone pitched in, and I would be sent out with a pitcher of ginger water to refresh the sweating hands. Then came the excitement of loading the hayrick full to bursting, and finally the straining gallop of the huge horses up the steep barn driveway to the dusty haymow where a little earlier we had amused ourselves on rainy spring days by jumping off the rafter supports into the soft bed.

In the fall there were the cattle drives, collecting the farmer's surplus and driving them along quiet dusty country roads to the junction yards, where they were loaded on freight cars, given their last water, and shipped off to Montreal. It was fun watching the men push the freight cars by hand to the loading chutes. After the cattle were loaded, they were picked up by the afternoon freight, and my father left that night on the passenger train for the city to attend the auction. This was a big event for us all because he always came back with a list of city things he had brought my mother, while for each of us he had some small gift which was highly prized. Shortly afterwards, various neighbor farmers would come to the door and they were taken into his office, where big Canadian bills exchanged hands; and then the men often had a short drink from a bottle of claret, which was kept locked in a tantalus just for such a solemn occasion. My mother, who was a strict teetotaler, disapproved of this, but my father would justify it on the grounds that it was a business necessity. I always loved the smell of my father's office, so masculine and forbidden, smelling of cigars and wine and money and all things wicked.

Living on an isolated farm and with no sisters to play with, I suspect, as I look back on my childhood, that I was a rather lonely girl. Nevertheless, I made up for this enforced solitariness by cultivating a rich fantasy life which included a number of imaginary playmates, especially my best friend Ida. I would go off with the dog to a secluded spot on the hill behind the farmhouse and sit down on some moss which had an overlook to the far-away mountains in the north. Then my little playmates would come, and we would spend hours together. I cannot remember now what we did or said, but I can remember that they were very comforting, and I never felt lonely when with them.

One lovely spring afternoon, when I was about eleven, I must have fallen asleep at such play, and I had a most curious dream. In it my imaginary playmate Ida came to see me, loving but sorrowful. She kissed me on both cheeks and, holding my hand, said: "Now I must leave you and go away forever, but before I go, I want to introduce you to a great lady." Then there was a tiny white ball far away, which rapidly approached, flying through the air and getting larger as it came. It came to rest in front of me; and, as it did, Ida disappeared, and out of the white ball stepped a gracious splendidly dressed lady, whom I instinctively trusted.

"My dear child," she said smiling at me all the while, but with a certain grave authority that I did not doubt, "Your childhood days are soon to end; and you will go away to great responsibilities which will increase as you grow older. My work is there for you to help me with, which you can do, for you have great talents just waiting to be developed. So keep a stout heart, do not ever be downcast, and persevere in all things. My strength will go with you and aid you in whatever you do."

She disappeared; and I woke up from this strange dream. But I never forgot it.

Our family was growing up — I, along with the rest, catching up with my older brothers, who were already young men. About fourteen, I began to take religion very seriously and was baptized and confirmed in the church. But I continued to be puzzled over why God permitted evil to exist.

At about this time, after much family prayer and consultation, I was sent away to a ladies' seminary in Gorham, Maine, run by my church. It had been decided after painful soul-searching that a young lady needed more culture and amenities than either the farm or the local school could provide. I was both terrified and at the same time delighted to be thus on my own, away from the strict discipline of my parents. I shall never forget awakening before dawn and being driven to Compton depot by my parents in the best family rig, and being put aboard the Grand Trunk morning train for Portland with all my luggage, and even a lunch box of food to comfort my journey. After being solemnly abjured under no conditions to talk with strangers, warned about the insidious wiles of white slavers, and being placed by my father under the special protection of the conductor, I timidly boarded, and we were off in a cloud of smoke and cinders.

After initial homesickness, I found the school a source of unbelievable freedom and cosmopolitan culture: It actually had young ladies from Boston and New York. But now, when I look back on it, I realize how circumscribed and stilted our education really was in the face of changes which were about to burst upon us. Impressed by my parents' sacrifice in sending me there, I determined to succeed. Needless to say I studied hard and liked the school very much. I persevered in my studies, especially in Latin and French, and received high marks. My parents were at first dubious about the latter subject, as it reminded them too much of the despised French "habitant" who formed our lower class. But I persuaded them that I was learning Parisian French, not habitant patois, and that the ladies from Boston and New York thought it was *comme il faut!*

I spent four very pleasant years at the seminary and graduated as class salutorian. Then the war broke out in the summer of 1914. Soon upon my visits back to the farm, it was strange to see my brothers in uniform, but even stranger to see a friend they had brought back with them from training camp. He was the handsomest young man I had ever seen, — tall, dark, with high cheek bones and a smooth face like a Greek god; I am afraid I fell madly in love with him on the spot. We were soon betrothed, and I shall never forget the sweet sadness of those far-off days, — love amid the knowledge that we were soon to be parted, perhaps forever. Surprisingly, my parents, usually so strict, while providing full chaperonage, did not in the least discourage the match; it seemed the young man's parents were wealthy ranchers in Alberta. But though we had several meetings at my home, the time inevitably came when they all had to leave for the front, and I had to go back to school. I had now been hired back at the seminary as an assistant language teacher, a job which I much enjoyed. I looked forward to staying at the school for the duration, and then marrying my young man and going to a new life in Alberta with him.

One midnight, some months later, I was awakened by an urgent telegram — an unheard-of procedure. COME AT ONCE: DEATH IN FAMILY it read. The milk train from Portland came by at 4:23 A.M. and I was on it, pale and shaken. The hired man was at the Compton station with a rig. His face was grim. One of my brothers and my fiancé had been killed in action; and my other brother was wounded. My mother had a heart attack upon hearing the news and had lapsed into a coma. My father was distraught and in no condition to leave the house.

One may well imagine the turmoil caused in my mind by these staggering, and unforeseen events, so violent and foreign to any of my previous experience. Nevertheless, it was instantly obvious that I was the one to take command of the situation, which I did at once, repressing my own strong feelings of remorse over the death of my beloved. The bodies were never recovered, so we could only have a memorial service. My mother never regained consciousness and died a few weeks later. My father was shattered in spirit and grew to be an old man before our eyes. He was no help at all in attending to farm affairs, so my presence was absolutely necessary to keep the remains of our family afloat. I had to resign my post at school, for my wounded brother was shortly discharged and remanded to our care. Fortunately, he recovered enough to be able to get around reasonably well, and eventually was able to take charge of matters on the farm, as well as to see after our father. All these events took a year or so, during which period, I had ample time for reflection.

Needless to say these tumultous events produced a crisis in my life and eventually a profound change in my thinking. I resolved I would not dispair, but I could not understand why such violence should happen to me. Why does God permit such evil to exist? Why are people allowed to get sick — to be blown to bits — to die lingering and painful deaths? I sought refuge in the Bible and reread *Job* carefully, seeking to find why wrath is permitted to be visited on a just man; but I found little enlightenment. Some key was necessary.

During my stay at the seminary, I had met another teacher who seemed to have some inkling of help for these hard questions, though at that time I was not at all willing to accept her theories. She was a Christian Scientist, and she said that in reality there was no evil — it was just an illusion which we allowed to happen because we did not "demonstrate" the truth. I neither understood nor believed her at the time; but in my present extremity, I was willing to grasp at anything which would help my predicament. I wrote her about it, and in reply she sent me a copy of *Science and Health* which I read with considerable interest. Never one to do things by halves, I decided I would try out this new doctrine. So when freed from my farm responsibilities, I emigrated to Boston and shortly afterwards joined the Mother Church. The change was therapeutic, and my morale improved. If it helped me this much, it would surely help others, and perhaps I could be part of that help. I decided to take a professional class in Christian Science practice and hopefully become a practicioner. I would devote my life to bringing this truth to other people so it could help them as it had helped me in overcoming deep sorrow and depression.

To support myself in these new surroundings, I got a job at the Christian Science Publishing Society, adjacent to the Mother Church, and worked in the MEW department. This was the oldest area of the business, consisting of the sale of Mary Baker Eddy's works, especially *Science & Health*. Many of the people who worked there had been her friends, proteges and retainers. They were full of reverent stories of the fabled founder of Christian Science, and from them I learned many anecdotes, not published, as well as some of the lore, not in official documents. I can still remember how on Fridays we were paid by a little old cashier who came around with a flimsy and delapidated cart-tray and handed us our wages to the penny in cash.

I also found a small apartment round the corner on Mass. Ave., nearly opposite the Philharmonic, so I got to it and the Pops often. I suppose the place is torn down now, but it was very convenient to the Fenway, to Mrs. Jack Gardner's, and the Boston Museum of Fine Arts. I loved the Italian Palace, and used to spend hours there at the the Fine Arts Museum, receiving from both places a liberal education in art, sculpture, and architecture, which I was not to have through travel. The Mass. Ave. cars went to Cambridge and Harvard, and the Huntington Ave. cars went downtown, as well as to Brookline, so I was very centrally situated for business or pleasure.

After the shock of losing my beloved fiance' I had decided never again to place my love in mortal man, but to devote my life to God; and consequently I did not date at all and confined my social life to female friends I met at the Publishing House. Fortunately there were enough of these for my meager needs; for, to tell the truth, my interest in the practice of Christian Science seemed to me to offer the only salvation both for me personally and for mankind in general.

Once I received my C.S.B. I devoted myself entirely to the practice of Christian Science and lived a nun-like life socially. I quickly found that I had indeed been granted the grace of healing by Christ Jesus and this without the laying on of hands, through absent treatment. I simply held the patient in my thoughts, saw him or her hale and whole, and loved by Christ and by myself. I concentrated on seeing the three of us, Christ, the patient, and myself, as together and at one in some mystic trinity, and my efforts seemed successful.

My practice, which had started small, grew rapidly larger, until I had necessarily to limit it, in order to devote more time to my studies and meditations. Needless to say, I became an avid student of Christian Science, as well as of the healing art in general. I became interested in how other religions and healing cults mirrored though imperfectly, the truths I had found in Christian Science. In this respect I was particularly interested in the healing arts of the Hawaiian Kahunas, with their three spirits — high, middle, and low — which, so nearly from a supposedly heathen culture mimicked our conception of Christ Jesus, mortal mind, and man's individual soul. While some of my fellows looked somewhat askance at my scholarly interest in these esoteric healing areas, I held fast to the central tenets of my faith; and did not deviate in the manner of Holmes of Religious Science or Fillmore of the Unity movement. Neither did minor arguments and schisms within the Church interest me. I was interested, however, in the Christian saints, particularly in their unsought-for ability to heal. Was this grace, I wondered, a special gift from Christ himself as a reward for their faith, or was it a natural accomplishment of their escalation? I read considerably in the lives of the Christian Saints, I was intrigued to learn how they had surmounted the difficulties of the Catholic religion. I grew more tolerant of Roman Catholicism upon being introduced to some of its major saints, especially as I remembered that in most of the time there was no Christian alternative. While these efforts were made without practical motive solely in the pursuit of an intellectual quest, they seemed to result in general improvement in my professional abilities, and I was faced with an embarrassment of riches in my practice. It henceforth became necessary to limit my services to certain types of cases.

I have found that repeating the *Scientific Statement of Being* over and over to myself with my eyes closed and otherwise being situated in an attitude of prayer can be very efficacious in bringing my mind to a state of calm and order. How long these reveries last I do not know; they can go on for half an hour or more. At such times, when I can completely shut out outside thoughts, I become insensible to external things and I find that, when this one-pointed concentration has been obtained and sustained, the gradual fusion of the ideal or perfect state of my patient in my mind together with this one-pointed calm produces the best demonstrations. For what manifests in the world of experience is a semblance of the original order or collectedness which is imminent throughout time and space on the ideal plane.

It is absolutely necessary to live a pure life in order to prepare the body to act as a proper vehicle to achieve these heights. It is necessary to eschew all negative emotions, especially hatred and violence. It is even wise to refrain from sex, the eating of meat, and the stressful incursions of daily media. But the challenge of the possibility of access to such high places has always been an objective; for the increased preview it gives one in the consciousness of the Divine is balm to the soul. I have, therefore, often persisted in such practice, though in some ways it has tended to estrange me from social life.

I am accustomed on these occasions of revery to see colors of wondrous beauty softly blending into one another as does the rainbow, though they have a quality of intensity that even the rainbow cannot match. Sometimes there are small lights like bright fireflies among the colors, and, of course, on some occasions there are no colors at all.

One day on which there had been more colors than usual and my mind was perfectly at peace, I was suspended in quiet contemplation like a light uniting all things when I saw a flash of wonderful splendor, different and more effulgent than any I had evern seen before. It unveiled itself as if it were a curtain parting to reveal a tableau on a stage. In the center of the radiance was a rainbow of lucent reflection and color and over it another of equal grandeur with the spectrum oppositely located as in a double natural rainbow. Above the arches stood the cross with a crown weighing on its crossbar. And within the arches shone the form of Christ Jesus himself.

It is an understatement to say that I was stupefied by this vision, so beautiful and so different from anything I had ever experienced before. It would be better to say that all thought of self was lost and I seemed to merge with the vision. In that timeless moment I recongized with a flash of illumination the gift had been given: That God is Love, that He is All, that there is nothing else, that sin and error do not exist, that ideally all men and women are whole and hale, that we are all immortal, that there need be no fear of death nor sin, and that the kingdom of heaven is here and now. But these statements are mere shadows of the compelling sense of truth that was instantaneously conveyed to me. This overpowering sense of God's goodness and love completely overcame me, and I was suffused with emotion — tears of joy ran down my face and I tried to prostrate myself from my sitting position to give proper homage to the Lord of Love. To my absolute amazement, I found that *I was up in the air, unsupported by anything!*

The minute I recognized this fact, I came down with a bump and fell over in a heap.

You may well imagine the reactions which this extraordinary experience produced in me. First there was the ineffable sense of calm and peace, something utterly too holy and sacred to describe. So I shall say no more about it. (It did produce, however, a burning curiosity to find out what others who had been granted such an experience felt about it afterward.) Second, it produced a profound cognitive curiosity as to the

128

mechanism and dynamics of levitation itself. While much still remained a mystery, the experience had clearly revealed several important facts:

1. The experience was real; the mystics and saints have not lied to us.

2. Since accompanied by such exalted visions and revelations of God and Christ Jesus, it is a holy experience (and not one produced by mesmerism, animal magnetism, or mortal mind), hence, worth of study repetition and research.

3. Since the experience occurs "naturally" (that is, without the wilful intent to produce by the participant), it must be explained as a product of natural law, rather than as a phenomenon induced by certain powers.

(Parenthetically, I may also state that the "demonstration" was complete and especially gratifying to the patient).

Since Christian Science teaches that God is understanding as well as love, I felt it incumbent upon me to seek understanding of the theophany which had happened to me; therefore, when other responsibilities did not intrude, I devoted myself to a study of levitation and its concomitants. Since that initial time, I have experienced levitation but rarely. It was always the accompanient of a very complete revery such as I have before described. And it also accompanies the best demonstrations, as if it were the epiphenomena of a complete loss of self in the Infinite. My efforts led me to a careful reading of the lives of Christian saints, and eventually Hindu yogis. I discarded accounts of all others such as mediums, shamans, etc., where other than Divine intervention might be inferred. What follows is necessarily a somewhat condensed and difficult treatise on a very rare phenomenon which attempts to look at levitation from the point of view of dynamics and to reconcile, if possible, the differences between Hindu levitation (as described by Patanjali) where levitation is sought as a siddhi or miracle, and Christian levitation (where it comes as unrequested epiphenomena to a profound mystic state of rapture).

I pondered about all this for a great while, but nothing that I read in sacred or profane scriptures seemed to help. Then I decided to make a demonstration about it, and go at it as if it were an illness instead of an ignorance. With this new tack the idea kept forming in my mind: "Whatever is God's will is completely natural, therefore look for that which is natural." I decided to look at natural law, especially law of physics, and to see if in some way they could be surmounted naturally. In this endeavor I was thinking of the way that progress and the understanding of Archimedes' principle of floating bodies finally allowed us to consider building iron boats instead of wooden ones, whereas before we had thought that we could not do so because iron sinks while wood floats.

One day I read a profound scientific book about Planck's quantum theory, and it was this idea which provided the breakthrough. There is no reason why the quantum theory cannot be applied to truth and error. So let us suppose that everything, including ourselves, is made up of quanta (or packets) of truth and packets of error, which can of course vary under diferent conditions. We will assume, for convenience, that the size of each of these packets is the same, so that what varies is the number of them. Let us also assume that through prayer, meditation or other "good works" the number of error packets or quanta can somehow be reduced or replaced with truth quanta. Now in general every system (and a system can be a human being) is made up of truth quanta and error quanta (some more or less of each), so that for every truth quanta there is an error quanta, etc.

[2]To reduce this scientific jargon to a more human situation, let us suppose that there is a band of Arabs, who wear nothing but sheets, as many as they own. They also are very democratic, so that the sheets are divided evenly insofar as that may be done. Viewed from a distance, all the Arabs will look alike. Now let the number of sheets somehow become less and less, until finally there are fewer sheets than Arabs. Now a strange thing happens. There are two kinds of Arabs — those with sheets and those who are naked. Their behavior will be rather different, and it will be easy to tell them apart.

If we let the sheets signify error packets or quanta and no sheets signify truth packets or quanta, then there can come a situation where there is so much order in a system that there are not enough error packets to go around, and consequently some part of the system is in a state of perfect order. A system in a state of complete order is not subject to ordinary laws of statistics; popularly we can say that this is when miracles occur.[2]

I'm not sure that this labored explanation of the order which may produce levitation will satisfy very many people, but I am perfectly convinced that levitation does occur under rare conditions. I also believe that, since it occurs, it must be possible to explain it, if we had the expanded views necessary to do so.

I do not regard it as any more of practical value than the curious behavior of helium when very near total order (absolute zero). But just as the superconductivity and superfluidity of helium reveals certian laws of nature hidden under more disordered conditions, so it seems to me that levitation and other "miracles" may be helpful in understanding the Divine nature of the world. Our efforts should center not on dwelling at conditions near absolute zero or the continual experience of levitation, but upon perfecting order in our lives, of which such effects are the merest epiphenomena. It is, after all, the journey itself which is the goal. Imagine

Heaven not as the hereafter but as a realm of perfected ideals, much as Plato did.

Let us further imagine that the true conception for each of us is a "glorious body" in that realm that is spoken of in the New Testament. Besides being perfect, imagine that this "glorious body" has all the properties of regularity and order as does a perfect crystal, so that it is at the same time both a human being and a crystal. Now imagine that it can vibrate and hence resonate with Cosmic Mind. When this happens, we see that everything true of Cosmic Mind is true of this body. Hence, sin, disease, and death become impossible in that realm.

Now imagine that deeds of merit in our life here help to create and embody this perfect being, though of course only in part. Especially efficacious in this process is meditation and the mental work of demonstration, which besides bringing the perfected body at least somewhat into consciousness, also in some other manner sets the crystal to vibrating. Creativity, healing and miracles are the inevitable result. They are not the fruits of petition; they occur naturally whenever the requisite conditions are present. Mrs. Eddy tells us to "rise in the strength of spirit." When our consciousness resonates with Infinite Mind, all things are possible. This is indeed what every higher religion has told us and what the New Testament says plainly. As Socrates put it: "Dwelling in that communion only, he would be able to bring forth not mere images of Beauty, but Beauty herself, and so to become immortal and to be the friend of God."

★   ★   ★

I have tried to explain in my own way an experience which may be ineffable. The Catholic saints say that it is a mystery or a grace and so defies natural logic. I'm not sure I can agree with them in this, but I am sure that any explanation takes a different kind of reasoning than most of us are familiar with. I suspect that, like the men in Plato's cave, we reason from familiar premises, which will prove upon further study to be specious. T.S. Eliot's little bird told us that "Human beings cannot stand much reality." and this may very well be why faith is such an important component of any religion. Naturally, I have a lot of faith. Whether you have will probably determine whether you can accept this testimony.

11 — MISS TENNOYER

[1]This story is based on a purportedly true incident reported to the author; the principal in the case when asked about it would neither confirm nor deny the facts. Levitation, however, has had a long and impeccably documented history, a summary account of which will be found in Gowan (1980:190-206). There have been three major manifestations, all well

attested: 1) those of Christian mystics (St. Francis, St. Teresa, St. Joseph of Cupertino, 2) those of western paragnosts of whom the best known was Home, and 3) those of recent date relating to the Transcendental Meditation siddhi. That these experiences are "real" in the sense that they are not mere OBE's or hallucinations can be seen from the fact that in each of the cases cited above they were observed by witnesses. Furthermore they were all levitations of the person, rather than that of objects, such as a handkerchief, candle or table. For further information and a theory as to the explanation for levitation, see (Gowan 1980:190-206).

★ ★ ★

This argument is simplified from (Gowan 1980:385-6).

CHAPTER 12
Egeria

My given name, Egeria, was the only pretense I had to elegance, for I was born shortly before WW2 on a small farm in a glen in the Great Smokies. The name had been given to me by my grandmother, who was to become such an important figure in my life, as indeed she was in our family. Outside of the fact that I had an older brother and a younger sister, I remember very little about my early home, for when I was still quite young, the War broke out, and my father enlisted, leaving the care of the farm to my mother and older brother. My mother's health had been impaired by too rapid child-bearing, and it was eventually decided that I should go and live with my grandmother. This fortitious change proved to have a major influence on my entire subsequent life.

My grandmother, who had just been widowed, was a strong matriarchal figure. She had come from a good family in Virginia, and had received a fair education, enough so that she could teach school. She loved books, almost as much as she loved flowers and plants. She gave me the love I needed, and together, with the aid of a hired man we ran the farm. We were inseparable. I remember tending the chickens, feeding the pigs, and pitching down hay for the horses. I also helped her tend a large kitchen garden, for we produced almost everything we ate. I even slept with grandmother, and used to feel the warmth of her body on cold winter nights. We were very compatible, and as I grew older, I realized that we were much alike; we both loved books, and learning, enjoyed and found solace in the outdoors and in nature and flowers, and used to go for walks in the piney woods.

Yes, I had imaginary playmates, but they were not of the ordinary kind. You see to me the "little people: — elves, fairies, nymphs, sylphs, all these were quite real. What I like about them most I think, was that you did not have to talk to them — they read your thoughts, and communicated with you the same way. I guess one reason why I liked flowers so much is that that is where the little people lived — in the flowers, the grass, and in trees. I can remember being absorbed for hours by the minutiae of nature — the glory in the flower — and by the spaciousness of the pure sky, merely because each of these offered a kind of freedom to be in touch with these spirits which nobody else seemed to see or place any value on. This was my private realm. I was the only human privy to its wondrous secrets. I could go there every afternoon after school and, once out of sight of others, I entered this enchanted fairyland where thoughts were things and all my fantasies came true. In this secret and wondrous realm I was the queen, and the fairies, nymphs and others would come willingly to me and do my bidding. They showed me the secrets of nature, and refreshed my childish soul with companionship and peace which I had never known from any other source.

I remember walking the country roads to school with my lunch box, thoughtfully packed each morning by grandmother. But grandmother was not satisfied with the learning I received there by itself and out of carefully saved egg money, I remember how she bought me twenty volumes of *The Book of Knowledge* and with what delight I poured over its treasured arcana of wonders. Soon I was introduced to the county library, especially the bookmobile which made bi-weekly visits to our school.

I did very well in my classes, but I was never one to associate very much with other children. Indeed, I felt no need, for I had my own coterie of imaginary playmates whom I used to visit every afternoon in a bosky dell behind our garden. Some teachers felt I was asocial, but it never seemed to bother me to be alone. I was considered a scholar and a "grind", and was never popular either with girls or boys. I tended to be skinny, and not especially pretty; at least I thought so, for my clothes, while good homemade items, were obviously not store-bought.

In high school I continued my academic excellence, especially in language arts and biology, though I did little at adolescence to enhance my social position. I was much too shy to date and still enjoyed a very close relationship with my grandmother. About this time I was molested by a young neighbor and, while not harmed, I was frightened by the act, and this made me shy away even more from contacts with males.

In my senior year at high school it became obvious that I should go to college, perhaps to become a biologist or a teacher. There was, however, not enough money for me to do so, and it was decided that I would go to Nashville and work in a cotton factory after graduation. I graduated as valedictorian of my class, but with no prospects of anything further. Then my grandmother had a heart attack and died immediately. Her entire estate, farm and all, was left to me provided I used the money to go to college. I eagerly complied with this last wish of my grandmother's and after the farm was shortly rented entered a residential college in

Kentucky.

I enjoyed my college years very much, though I had to supplement my meager funds by working as a waitress in the dorm. I was still shy of social contacts, but spent all my energies in study motivated by gratitude for my grandmother's sacrifice. I saw less and less of my own family, who were now like strangers, further removed by the fact that they had been cut out of grandmother's will. I found myself writing poetry and became a contributor to the college publications. With little social or athletic life, I was a rather typical university intellectual. I idolized my professors, constantly asking them extra questions about my studies, and found in most of them a great willingness to oblige the curiosity of a student.

While not interested in competitive athletics, I did find, because of my love of the outdoors, a great interest in hiking and mountaineering. I even joined a club interested in such activities, and it proved to be an excellent outlet for my physical energies and needs.

The outing club also filled a need I had for social companionship with men. The unit consisted of about twice as many men as women, so we girls had to be rugged and have a lot of stamina for we were expected to carry our packs and endure the hard climbs along with the men. A camaradie, however, inevitably developed between the men and girls; although our dating was almost inevitably in multiples and, at least as far as I was concerned, nothing more than a few good-night kisses ever eventuated even on our overnight hikes. I do remember, however, being approached one night in our tent by another girl who wanted to cuddle naked with me; I felt this was not right for me, and told her so. She never bothered me again. All in all, the outing club was a great experience for me, bringing me in contact with types of men I would never have otherwise met, and giving me both poise and understanding in dealing with them with friendliness and not fear.

As my senior year approached, it became more and more obvious that I was fitted to be a naturalist, for I came to be more and more engrossed in this area; even my poetry was about nature. One of my professors, who took an interest in me, got me a job after graduation as a naturalist graduate assistant in a nearby university, studying particularly the flora peculiar to this part of the United States. I was overjoyed, for I was never happier than when in outdoor clothes, working with nature.

A group of us had set out from Deepgap to spend a day tramping in the national forest trails. The hardwoods had just begun to turn, and their beautiful yellows and reds were contrasted with the green of the pine forest. [1]I was in good health and robust training and felt no thirst hunger or fatigue, — a state of peace and order with the world and myself.[1] [2]Suddenly and without any warning, an invisible curtain seemed to be drawn across the sky, changing the light and transforming the

135

environment into a kind of tent of enhanced significance. The outside became an inside and the objective, subjective.[2] I motioned the others to go on, but sat down on a rock to steady myself and recover my composure. Looking up, I found myself by a mountain pool, with shafts of light trickling down through the saffron trees to reveal the azure sky above. A ray of sunlight touched the pool with liquid gold, and dazzled my eyes. [3]Suddenly the world was mine, but in a way that "mine" had never meant before, for it embraced all humans. The pool became transparent to its green depths and I was plunged into those depths and yet lifted up with joy on the rising wind. The light intensified and changed its brilliance to a blinding white, in whose crystal purity there was a kind of ecstasy.[3] The presence of the Lord came over me; my soul knew His touch and it awakened. He made it bloom and blossom and I was enveloped in glory.

Against the light a duck flew in; [3]it seemed made of rhythm as it settled in the pool, with a strange kind of meaning to me that my emotions understood, but my mind did not. There was the same mystic meaning in the dragonfly, the moss, and the acorns which fell from the trees. And still the apperception grew and the significance. The significance was bliss, which made a created whole out of everything I watched and the essence of this creation was love. Love poured from the light, bathing me in music and with perfume. Love was the source of the light and yet the object of it. Love and the whole world were one.[3]

[4]There was nothing and no one whom I did not love at that moment, for the whole world was wrapped in inexpressible glory, and its waves of beauty and joy kept swelling and breaking on all sides. The sorrows, tensions, and fears, even of death, which had lain on my heart for so many years, were pierced and purged by this radiant effulgence. I seemed to witness in the wholeness of my vision the movements of all humanity, and to feel the beat of music and the rhythm of a mystic dance. I was conscious of an unutterable stillness and peace in my heart, and simultaneously every object about me seemed bathed in a soft lambent glow, purer, and more ethereal than I had ever sensed before.[4]

[5]Then words like a voice seemed to form in my mind, "God is all; He is not far away in the heavens; He is here. The grass under your feet is His bountiful harvest. The trees above your head, the blue sky, the pool, the mountains, you, yourself, as all one with Him. All is well, for ever and ever, for there is no place nor time where God is not. And you yourself, as are all humankind, the most beautiful and wonderful expressions of His love. Then the earth, air and sky thrilled and vibrated to this one celestial song, and the theme of it was "Glory to God in the highest, peace and good will toward all persons".[5]

[6]There came to me in clearer form than ever before the continual

sanctity of nature, from the smallest thing to the largest creature, and the particular value of human life as having dominion over this paradise. There was an instinctive awe, mixed with delight and even glee in this wondrous universe, and an indefinable thrill, such as we sometimes imagine to indicate the presence of a disembodied spirit. I still, shiver from head to foot with the joy and fear of it.[6]

[7]Then slowly the glorious ecstasy left my heart, for I felt that God had withdrawn His presence and the communion which He had granted. I was able to rise again and walk on, very slowly, so strongly was I still possessed by this strange interior emotion. The state of rapture might have lasted four or five minutes, though at that time it seemed much longer. But my personality had been transformed by the presence of the living spirit. God's presence was there, though invisible. I apprehended Him by none of my senses, yet my consciousness perceived His presence.[7] [8]That the experience was not just a passing fancy, but an intimation of immortal life, I had recognized in a flash of illumination. I also realized that it had not been an idle gift, but had been offered for some deep purpose. A curtain hitherto unnoticed had suddenly been flung aside and, though other veils intervened, for one timeless moment there stood partly revealed to me the ineffable and stunning mystery of life. I was awed by this relevation of love. Then the curtain fell again, and I perceived "the glory fade into the light of common day.[8]

Then something really eerie happened. I sensed, rather than heard, a strange voice inside me singing God's praises, but in a tongue unknown to me. This mysterious inner chant went on for some time, and I cried with the bliss and the perfection of it.

I sensed that I had been assured that I was God's special child, and that, as such, I had powers and abilities I had not exercised. Rather than being elated by this relevation, I felt humbled and concerned to discharge this enlarged responsibility. No such privilege as I had been afforded is without its duty. It was my task to discern this duty clearly and to carry it out, with the renewed confidence and enhanced self-concept which had been so generously afforded me.

[5]I soon rejoined my friends, who had grown somewhat concerned about me. They all remarked a shining change in my face, and they asked what had happened to me. I was unable to tell them. An infinite joy and peace filled my heart. Worldly ambitions and cares vanished in the light of the glorious truth which had been revealed to me. All anxiety and concern about the future utterly left me, and my life seemed one long song of peace and love. It was as if I had somehow merged with all nature in a total unity with all that is.[5] I felt that I was in complete harmony with universal pure energy, but in some sort of a latent or at rest stage. It was a kind of transport, not beyond anything, but into anything that is.

Afterwards, I was filled with a calm and peace beyond understanding. In this calm, I realized that it was now my task to unleash this creative energy and to use it usefully in the world.

Somehow, I felt that if I went back on my grandmother's farm and lived for a while the life of a rustic hermit, future steps in my life might become more clear. It was obvious that I loved nature and was fitted to be a naturalist, but how could I best accomplish the fullness I wanted from life within this discipline?

I meditated and wrote in my journal on these matters, and in a short time it became clear to me that conservation of natural resources was a strong avenue of interest for me. I acquired some literature on the subject and attended conservation meetings and took extension courses. Next, I decided to apply for one of the forestry conservation jobs available at the National Park's Service. Having studied this area considerably, as well as being familiar with all the local flora, I passed both my oral and written examinations with high marks and was duly accepted into the service. Fortunately, I was assigned to a mountain park, rather near my grandmother's farm, so that I was able to live there and commute to work. I found this work very satisfying, particularly as I was able to concentrate on the conservation of rare local wild flowers. I began a seedling garden at the farm to propagate these plants more abundantly and then to transplant them to favorable wild habitats. I seemed to have a green thumb in these matters and my wildflower garden became locally well-known.

But more publicity was necessary, and I began to realize that I needed to write about these matters, the kind of popular pieces that local country newspapers would use as filler, thereby sensitizing their readers to the need for conservation of such species. I used a practical approach, stressing the natural herbal and curative properties of some of these plants, as well as their aesthetic appeal.

As a result of these efforts, which were rather popular in rural areas, I was forced to start an herb garden, and, as I would not take money for the herbs, I became rather busy in answering the constant demands of sick country folk for herbal remedies. I never prescribed; I simply gave people what they asked for.

With all these activities, plus a few farm animals to care for, I had a full life but more was to be added. Since I had often been alone as a child, I had never felt the pangs of loneliness on the farm, — at least so long as I kept busy. As a result, I had not dated and tended to live a hermit-type life, not avoiding the company of men, but not wearing rouge or lipstick, and usually appearing in boots and outdoor rough clothes all of which were entirely appropriate for the kind of work in which I was engaged. My face was sun-tanned and my hands often cracked with work and soiled with loam. I would often appear in public thus, when I took my column on nature in to the local newspaper.

One occasion in the Spring stands out in my mind. A young agricultural agent from Washington was coming to speak to a group of us on conservation of natural resources. While I was much interested in his topic, I do not remember anything else which gave intimation as to the future importance of the occasion. I do remember that I was seated in the back row of a tiered lecture room ready to take notes. The speaker, whose name was William Blake, was personable and attractive, and something about his ideas captured me at once. They seemed to be my own, coming back, better phrased and footnoted, as Emerson said "With a certain alienated majesty". I could not believe that another person could think so like myself. I was captivated. Although I am a very shy person, I could not restrain myself from going up afterwards to talk with him privately. He seemed also interested in me and in a longish talk I told him — I do not know why — of my own creative nature writing. I was astonished when he asked me if I would like to bring it to his room, and show it to him after lunch. I could not believe he had no ulterior motive.

Ordinarily I would have refused such an invitation out of hand, since I have been brought up never to visit a man's room; but for some reason I heard myself saying that I would come; I was mesmerized. Afterwards I died a thousand deaths, asking myself "What have I done? What has happened to me? Why am I behaving like a school girl?" I will never forget the trauma of walking up those stairs and knocking on that door at 2 pm. But somehow I did. There he was and behind him a big omnious double bed. Swallowing an impulse to run, I somehow entered and he closed the door.

If this were fiction, I would here interpose a romantic episode, in which I was swept into Bill's arms, but actually nothing of this kind happened, although we did have a long talk about how the aims of conservation could be forwarded by various writing efforts in different kinds of media. I finally left, ashamed of my fears, and reassured that there were men who respected women for their ideas. Nevertheless, I did realize that if he had tried to kiss me, I would not have resisted. I invited him to my house for supper, and to my surprise he said he would come. There seemed to be some kind of understanding between us.

★　★　★

I had fallen in love before, but meeting Bill was the weirdest experience in my life. Somehow I instinctively knew when I saw him that I belonged to him. He seemed to understand it himself; he simply came and took charge of me. My body knew his touch and awakened. The

Chinese have a proverb about it: "An affinity is predestined from a previous existence." That's the only rational way to explain it: we took up from where we had left off in lives beforehand.

All Bill had to do was to lay a hand on me, and I was ready for him. I am not that kind of girl, and it used to make me so mad, embarrassed and ashamed. And when I would blush and protest, he would simply touch me and show me the evidence. My body had betrayed me again. I would be mortified to death. How dare he know he could do that? If anyone else had ever tried such an unheard-of liberty, I would have been apoplectic, but Bill simply claimed what was already his. I never could make even the slightest resistance, because his touch mesmerized me; and once he touched me I started quivering, and from then on, it was one joyful road to ecstasy. I was enveloped in glory. I found to my wonderment that my body had longed all my life for his embrace.

He had another little habit of sidling up behind me, and, cuddling my neck with his right arm, thrusting his hand into my bodice, and cupping my left breast. He would gently squeeze the nipple till I would grow dizzy with pleasure. I could no more have stopped him than I could have stopped an avalanche. I would have been furious with anyone else trying such a stunt; but, with him, it seemed so warm and natural that I would lean back against him and want it to go on for ever. It was uncanny the power he wielded over me.

★   ★   ★

Needless to say, Bill and I were married shortly thereafter, and we decided to go back and make my grandmother's farm our headquarters. In connection with the farm, she had owned a sizeable piece of back woods and swamp land, which was generally considered good for nothing. A power project, however, wanted the land to impound water for a dam, and we received a rather handsome settlement when it was condemned for public use. With this largess, we decided to make a go of things on our own, using the farm as a base of operations. Naturally, this was not accomplished immediately. Bill gave up his job first to devote himself to fixing things up, while I remained in my naturalist role in the forestry corps. Shortly afterward, we were approached by some advocacy groups for conservation, and joined forces with them, using our farm as headquarters. Both Bill and I retained consultancy roles, travelling and speaking for a more humane and sane use of our natural resources, and meanwhile keeping up writing, and our flower and herbal gardens. It is a large task, but we are happy in it, and feel a completeness in our lives together.

For notes to this chapter see page 145.

5 — ANNE

To the pure all things are pure. To others, according to their deserts . . . To some these notes will seem prurient, to others, hallowed. For they attempt to show the almost embarrassing similarity between sexual and religious ecstasy. This relationship has been a source of confusion to the pious for years, and a soft point which critics of mysticism never tire of prodding. But it will be here suggested that not only is there a "big brother" relationship between the various kinds of ecstasy, but that sexual union is a literal and physical prefigurement of the divine union. Note the meaning of the prayer in the Angelican marriage service:

Oh, God, who has consecrated the state of matrimony to such an excellent mystery that in it is *signified and represented* the spiritual union between Christ and his Church.

For centuries men looked at the sun and did not realize that it had a beautiful and sizeable corona: the lesser effect was blotted out by the greater. There is an analog to this situation in the descriptions of sexual passion given by women (not men). When we read these accounts for the first time, we may be pruriently titillated, but if so we may miss the nuance of something important. Below are several protocols collected from women in regard to sexual bliss. It may be necessary for men to read them over several times in order to let the sexual excitement they normally engender to dissipate.

One cannot help being struck by the remarkable similarity between the outbursts of an impassioned woman and those of mystics recalling rapture. Both reveal a very similar ecstasy. First the former:

When you penetrate me, I feel as though I am consumed by God himself. The power, the strength, the only force that can harness and control my wild energy. And when I'm finally conquered, I scream out, "Oh, My God!" I submit and fall into sweet, sweet calm and peace. "Oh my stabilizer, my God, I love you my dearest!!"

★　★　★

Loving you, being loved by you, and celebrating that love through sexual intercourse, — that is to me beyond all gladness, all pleasure, all need and all desire and is the single most sacred act of my life. The point when you penetrate me and I am lost to all else but your literally being a part of me transcends life itself, and transports me as close as a mortal can come to be in touch with God. Because of that exquisite and direct experience of union with the Divine Nature of the universe, is the reason why I want and need to hold you in me, — why I want to stay in the deep, intimate sexual contact and union where is no differentiation between body and soul.

★　★　★

If a man were to write about these intimate matters, he would probably mention the mounting and physical mastery of the woman, the pleasure of thrusting into her, and the ecstasy of ejaculation. It is worthwhile to notice that none of these subjects are emphasized by women respondents. Instead they emphasize:

a) the act of penetration which completes some mystic connection,

b) the religious and theophanic overtones of the act,

c) the wholeness of "holding" the male organ within them,

d) the bliss, beyond "time, space and personality, and akin almost to union with the Deity,"

e) the loss of differentiation of self and other — "one flesh,"

f) the prolongation of the contact, rather than the orgiastic release.

Let is now turn to accounts of saints in holy ecstasy. It is no secret that church authorities have been embarrassed for centuries by the frankly sexual flavor of some of these protocols. But before we prejudge, let us respectfully remember that some of the holiest and saintliest of women are involved in these disclosures.

Our first holy witness is St. Marguerite Marie (Leuba 1925) as quoted by Gowan (1975-277):

One day as the Bridegroom was crushing her by the weight of his love and she was remonstrating, He said: "Let me do my pleasure. There is time for everything. Now I want you to be the plaything of my love, and you must live thus without resistance, surrendered to my desires, allowing me to gratify myself at your expense."

★   ★   ★

Our second, St. Teresa: (Gowan 1975:369):

It was the Lord's will that I should see an angel . . . I saw in his hand a long spear of gold, and at the iron's point there seemed to be a little fire. He appeared to me to be thrusting it time, and time again into my heart, and to pierce my very entrails. When he drew it out, he seemed to draw them out also and to leave me all on fire with a great love of God. The pain was so great that it made me moan, and yet so surpassing was the sweetness . . . that I could not wish to be rid of it.

★   ★   ★

Again. St. Teresa speaks of spiritual marriage, using the third person: (Gowan 1980:257):

To this person. . . the Lord revealed himself . . . when she had just received Communion, in great splendor, and beauty and majesty, . . . and told her it was time she took upon her His affairs as if they were her own, and that He would take her affairs upon Himself; and he added other words which are easier to understand than to repeat . . . For you must understand that there is the same difference between Spiritual Betrothal and Spiritual Marriage as there is between two betrothed persons and two who are united so that they cannot be separated any more.

★   ★   ★

The Passion of St. Therese of Lisieux is described (Gowan 1975:370):

I was in the choir . . . when suddenly I felt myself wounded by a dart of fire so ardent, I thought I should die. But what fire — what sweetness. Flames of love.

★   ★   ★

Many more illustrations could be adduced, but there seemes no point in laboring the issue. Instead we quote Underhill (1911:89) who summarizes:

"Attraction, desire, and union as the fulfillment of desire: this is the way Life

142

works in the highest and in the lowest things. The mystics' outlook indeed is the lover's outlook. It has the same element of wildness, the same quality of selfless and quixotic devotion, the same combination of rapture and humility. This parallel is more than a pretty fancy: for mystic and lover upon different planes, are alike responding to the call of the Spirit of Life. The language in which the passion is tepid and insignificant beside the language in which the mystics try to tell us of the splendors of their love. They force upon the unprejudiced reader the conviction that they are dealing with an ardor far more burning for an Object far more real. "This Monk can give lessons to lovers!" exclaimed Arthur Symons in astonishment of St. John of the Cross. It would be strange if he could not; since their finite passions are but the feeble images of his infinite one. . .

★ ★ ★

Those of us so weak we cannot fully love God, can at least love someone created in His image and likeness. While this love is earthly and hence physical in great part, it partakes somewhat of the celestial love of which it is a prefiguration. It is far more noble than the love of money, of fame, of power, or of food; it tends to refine and ennoble and to prepare one for sacrifice of the "little ego" and for the loss of selfhood which must accompany, (so the saints all tell us), the ultimate destiny of humanity.

★ ★ ★

[1]Adapted from Isherwood, M. *Root of the Matter*. London: Gollancz, as quoted by Happold (1963:129-30).
[2]From James, W. *Varieties of Religious Exlerience* as quoted by Happold (1963:139).
[3]From Gowan (1975:358) quoting Rufus Jones, *Studies in Mystical Experience* London: MacMillan (1932:196-7).
[4]From Underhill (1911:286).
[5]Adapted from Underhill (1911:293) quoting in translation Blessed Angela of Foligno.
[6]Adapted from Allen, W. *The Timeless Moment* quoted by Happold (1963:123).
[7]From R. Jefferies, *Story of My Heart* as quoted by E. Underhill, (1911:249).
[8]From Th. Traherne *Centuries of Meditations* as quoted by Happold (1963:368).

---

6 — MARIE

[1]This story is unlike others in the book as being a factual acccount of an experience of the author's when he was a university professor . . . Like the reader he looked for comfirmatory evidence. The book *Ye Are Gods,* an underlined copy of which was given him by Marie is still in his possession. It is instructive first to quote from some of the markings, a few of which seem especially relevant:

(p58-9): Our every thought must become a purpose, and that one great purpose must be to become like our Heavenly father . . . As one learns to become a musician by many hours of concentrated practice, so it is possible to control one's thoughts by so many hours of definite work. Just the desire and the will to practice brings the most astonishing results . . . When one learns to control thought, it becomes a simple thing to weigh every angle of the problems confronting one seeing its difficulties, its hopeless aspects even its utter impossibilities, its unsolved conditions. Then it will be possible to turn off the record, to relax the mind, and to go to sleep in peace, knowing with confidence that it will be solved. As one commands one's mind to relax, after giving the subject very careful thought from every angle, it is possible to turn the difficulty over to the subconscious mind for solving, which in turn has the power to reach out into the realms of Divine Light and receive answers. The most glorious thing is the amazing thoroughness of such a process, and the ease with which the difficulty is completely taken care of.

(p 69) (N.B. No underlining here, but on the margin of the page appears the comment in italics). *What are the elements a human uses for the fulfullment of the destiny or vision locked within?* Planting is done by holding thoughts in deep intensity until they are dropped into the realm of the emotions. This is conception . . . When thought and emotion are mingled the thought is conceived and will come forth. When they connect with the feeling, or emotions they become living vibrations, generated into growth and power, expanding into life. The point where thought and emotion meet is the place where vibration is released, and vibration is life.

(p 146) Vibration is the eternal actual substance of existence . . . We are no more than the thoughts we hold and the vibrations we send out into the universe.

(p 158) Light is the full perfection of all vibration . . . We will be astonished to find that it is not what we have done, . . . but what we are (N.B. added marginally *the completed vibration*). Learn to control vibrations by controlling thought and you hold the keys to eternal life . . . Light and Life and love and energy are the eternal elements and are vibrations created by mental thinking.

★ ★ ★

In some ways, this underlined material (only a fraction of which I have just quoted) was the most persuasive of all. It showed that somebody, putatively Marie, had studied the Skarin book with great diligence and attention, and had practiced and absorbed its teachings. As it happened none of the quoted material referred to translation directly, though the book has some passages which indicate that when the vibration is complete translation will occur. It was interesting to me that none of the underlined material referred specifically to Mormon doctrines or to the Christian Trinity, though there was plenty of such prose in the book itself. Furthermore the concept of thought and emotion as producing healing vibration is in line with many other esoteric teachings, notably those of Troward (1909) the Kahuna religion (Long 1945) and a number of Eastern sources. Indeed, several noted composers had noted that vibration preceded their best creative efforts (Gowan 1978). Whoever underlined the book was certainly not psychotic, but in full use of faculties, and obviously interested in self-actualization.

Not satisfied with a mere examination of the Skarin book, I commenced a wide study of translation and allied phenomena, which fell in line with a book that I was preparing, Gowan (1975). This subject proved exceedingly difficult to research, but after lengthy search, I did discover some material on it. I quote a paragraph, Gowan (1980:188):

Translation, "to convey or remove to heaven without death" is mentioned in the Old Testament in connection with Elijah and Enoch. While Elijah was purportedly carried to heaven in a chariot, the translation of Indian saints seems to take place in a flash of light. John (1978:242-3) describes the translation of Chaitanya, Jnanehwar, Tukarum and Ramalingam. Mohammed is believed by Muslims to have been translated. Some Christians believe that the shroud of Turin was caused by the translation of Jesus' body into a flash of light. We append the account of the translation of Tukarum as typical (*ibid:*273):

Tukarum sang late into the night: 'I have seen my own death with my own eye. It was inconceivably holy.' At the peak of his ecstasy, a blinding blaze of light caused his followers to close their eyes. When they looked again, Tukaram was gone.

Skarin (1952:183) quotes the *Apocrypha* as declaring that one "Tekla, a convert of Paul's was translated because of the righteousness of her life." And she further states that "the early saints were quite familiar with this power," naming John, the Beloved, and others.

I would now like to quote a few excerpts from *The Urantia Book* published anonymously in 1955 by the Urantia Foundation in Chicago. From page 622:

Such a morontia temple serves as the place of assembly for witnessing the translation of living mortals to the morontia existence. It is because the translation temple is composed of morontia material that it is not destroyed by the blazing glory of the consuming fire which completely obliterates the physical bodies of those mortals who experience final fusion . . .

From page 1212:

This fusion during physical life instantly consumes the material body. The human beings who might witness such a spectacle would only observe the translating mortal disappear in "chariots of fire."

* * *

There are also allied cases of Hindu yogis who have developed the power to impose the body at the time of death. So this matter is not merely an artifact of sectarian one, but a much more esoteric and widespread religious practice. Further curious information comes from the spontaneous human combustion deaths, popularly known as (Gowan 1980:162ff). One of the most curious aspects of such deaths in which most of body is consumed is that little else is burned. We do not have the space here for investigation of SHC, but one possible explanation is that there is a flash of light which lasts enough to consume the torso, but not long enough to set fire to the surroundings. We quote from writings elsewhere (Gowan 1980:165):

Rama (1978:449ff) devoted a chapter to yogic methods of "casting off the body," which include a) allowing oneself to freeze to death while in samadhi, retaining the breath under water, c) consciously opening the fontanelle at top of head, d) taking the body of another (p. 454ff), and e) spontaneous human combustion, about which Rama (1978:452) remarks:

There is another very rare way of casting off the body. By meditating on the solar plexus, the actual internal flame of fire burns the body in a fraction of a second, and everything is reduced to ashes. This knowledge was imparted by Yama, the king of death to his beloved disciple Nachiketa, in the *Kathopanishad.* Now all over the world, instances of spontaneous combustion are often heard about, and people wonder about such occurrences. But the ancient scriptures, such as *Mahakala Nidhi* explain this method systematically.

---

12 — EGERIA

[1]Happold (1963:139) quoting Wm. James *Varieties of Religious Experience.*
[2]Happold (1963:130) quoting Margaret Isherwood *Root of the Matter.*
[3]Happold (1963:90) quoting Anya Seton *The Winthrop Woman.*

[4]Happold (1963:140) quoting C.F. Andrews, quoting Tagore.
[5]Bucke, (1923:358) quoting C.Y.E.
[6]Gowan (1975:359) quoting Otto (1928:221) quoting Allen, quoting J. Ruskin.
[7]Happold (1963:139) quoting Wm. James (see [1]).
[8]Gowan (1974:114) quoting Blofeld (1970:23).

REFERENCES

Blofeld, J., *The Tantric Mysticism of Tibet.* New York: E.P. Dutton, 1970.

Boisen, A.T., *The Exploration of the Inner World.* New York: Harpers, 1936.

Bucke, M., *Cosmic Consciousness.* New York: Dutton. 1901, 1923.

Glashow, S.L., *Science* 210, 1319-1323 (1980).

Goldhaber, M., Langacker, R. & Slansky, R. *Science* 210, 851-860 (1980).

Gowan, J.C., *Trance, Art & Creativity.* Buffalo, NY: Creative Education Foundation,

Gowan, J.C., *Operations of Increasing Order.* (J.C. Gowan, 1426 Southwind Cir., We
    Village, CA 91361), 1980.

Gowan, J.C., "Creative Inspiration in Composers" in Gowan, J.C., Khatena, J
    Torrance, E.P., (Eds.) *Creativity: Its Educational Implications.* Dubuque, IA: Ke
    Hunt, Publishing Co., 1981.

Gowan, J.C., *Development of the Psychedelic Individual.* Buffalo, NY: Creative Educ
    Foundation, 1974.

Graef, Hilda. *Mystics of Our Times.* New York: Paulist Press, 1962.

Happold, F.C., *Mysticism.* Baltimore: Penguin Books, 1963.

Huxley, A. *The Perennial Philosophy.* New York: Harper Bros. 1945.

Jaynes, J., *The Origin of Consciousness in the Breakdown of the Bicameral Mind.* B
    Houghton-Mifflin, 1976.

John, Bubba Free, (Franklin Jones), *The Paradox of Instruction.* San Francisco: The
    Horse Press, 1977.

Long, Max F., *The Secret Science Behind Miracles.* Marina del Ray, CA: deVorss
    1954.

Rama, Sri Swami. *Living with the Himalayan Masters.* Honesdale, PA: Hima
    International Inst. Press, 1978.

Salam, A., *Science* 210, 723-32, 1980.

Skarin, Annalee. *Ye Are Gods.* New York: Philosophical Library, 1952.

Troward, Th., *The Edinburgh Lectures.* New York: Dodd & Mead, 1909.

Underhill E., *Mysticism.* London: Methuen & Co., 1911.

Weinberg, S., *Science* 210, 1212-18, 1980.

Zukav, B., *The Dancing Wu Li Masters.* New York: Wm. Morrow & Co., 1979.

anonc

tr
tc
g
tl
!

h
i

i
decoi
doctri
confir
SHC
the b
invest
long e
Again

b
b)
to
cc

DATE DUE
